THE WALTHAMSTOW CHARITIES

$\Longleftarrow\!\!\!-\!\diamond\!-\!\!\Longrightarrow$

Caring for the Poor 1500-2000

Above left. Removal Order. *Above right*. Bastardy Examination paper. *Above*. Application vouchers for coal.

THE WALTHAMSTOW CHARITIES

Caring for the Poor 1500-2000

James M. Gibson

Phillimore

2000

Published by
PHILLIMORE & CO. LTD.,
Shopwyke Manor Barn, Chichester, West Sussex
in association with the Walthamstow Almshouse and General Charities
and the Walthamstow Historical Society

ISBN 1 86077 154 8

Printed and bound in Great Britain by
BOOKCRAFT LTD.,
Midsomer Norton, Bath

Contents

List of Illustrations

Frontispiece: Documents from the archives of St Mary's Church
and the Walthamstow Charities

Acknowledgements

The Trustees of the Walthamstow Almshouse and General Charities have provided financial support during the research and writing of this history and granted access to their historical and current records. Mrs. Violet Smith, Mrs. Janet Lewis, and the Rev. Paul Butler, members of the trustees' book committee, and Ed Snowdon, clerk to the trustees, have offered their advice and support. The Walthamstow Historical Society, and in particular Philip Plummer and Mrs. Winifred Ellingham, have advised on publishing arrangements and undertaken the local marketing of the book. At the Waltham Forest Archives and Local Studies Library, the Archivist, Josephine Parker, and the Local Studies Librarian, Brian Mardall, have produced many books and documents and patiently answered many questions. Vestry House Museum has supplied photographs from its collection for some of the illustrations. The British Library has granted permission to reproduce the sketch of the Sir George Monoux Almshouses from Add. Ms. 18783. Photography for the dust jacket and the remaining illustrations has been provided by Ann-Marie Coxon. The author wishes to thank all of these people and organisations who have made this book possible.

Introduction

Walthamstow in 1500

A T THE BEGINNING OF THE 16TH CENTURY, Walthamstow, a small rural
village clustered around the parish church of St Mary, contained only 99 people
assessed for the lay subsidy granted to Henry VIII by Parliament in 1523-4.[1] Surrounding
the village among the woodland and pastures and fields worked by peasants and
labourers stood the ancient manor houses occupied by the great lords of the manor
and the modern villas occupied by wealthy London merchants. The contrast between
the rich and the poor was sharp and unforgiving; the sources of charity were few,
relying to a great degree on the generosity of the great and the good.

During medieval and early modern times the poor traditionally relied on three
sources of charity—the family, the manor, and the monastery—and the Walthamstow
poor were no exception. The family formed the first line of defence against poverty,
parents caring for children and grandchildren and children supporting parents and
grandparents, in extended families that did not move far from their place of birth nor
far from the churchyard where their ancestors lay buried.

When disease or desertion, death or disaster breached that first fortification, the
poor fell back on the generosity of the lord of the manor for their subsistence. Since
the early middle ages the manor had formed a self-sustaining economic unit, villeins
and serfs providing labour and service for the manorial lord in return for economic
security and protection. In his turn the manorial lord provided service for the great
barons and the king in return for their protection and defence against enemies and
invaders. Domesday Book lists two manors in Walthamstow: Hecham (Higham) in the
northern part of the parish, held by Peter de Valognes; and Wilcumestou (Walthamstow)
in the southern part of the parish, held by Ralph de Toni, who had married Judith,
niece of William I.[2] By the beginning of the 16th century the manor of Walthamstow
had been divided into the manor of Walthamstow Toni or High Hall containing land
in the south-east corner of the parish, the Rectory manor containing land near the
church given to the Priory of Holy Trinity Aldgate in the 12th century, and the manor
of Walthamstow Francis or Low Hall containing land in the south-west corner of the

parish. To the north the manor of Higham had also been divided into the manors of Higham Benstead and Salisbury Hall.[3] All the land in Walthamstow, then, was distributed among these five manors, leased to tenants on copyhold leases, and administered through the respective manorial courts. If a tenant were very wealthy and the lord of the manor were willing, he could enfranchise his land, purchasing the freehold and freeing it from manorial control. At the bottom of the economic structure, however, the poor peasants and labourers, who went with the land could only rely on the generosity of their manorial court officials and manorial lords for subsistence when too old or sick to work.

The last line of defence for the poor, when forced off the land and reduced to begging, was the charity of the church dispensed at hundreds of monasteries that dotted the countryside during the medieval period. Every monastery had an almoner, a monastic official responsible for distributing bread and alms at the monastery gates. Within the monastery there was usually also an almonry near the church of the monastery, which offered hospitality to homeless travellers or care for the sick. Larger monasteries often established hospitals for longer term care of the old and infirm, the lame and the blind. At the beginning of the 16th century, however, the nearest monasteries to Walthamstow were the ancient Benedictine nunnery of Barking Abbey, founded in 666; the hospital at Ilford, founded in the 13th century to care for the poor suffering from leprosy; and the richest monastic house in Essex, the Augustinian Abbey of Waltham Holy Cross.[4]

Closer to home, the parish church of St Mary may have offered some occasional relief to the poor, but no churchwardens' accounts survive from this early period. The churchwardens did, however, administer one small charity given by the Rev. William Hyll, vicar of Walthamstow from 1470 to 1487. By his Will dated 17 May 1487, the Rev. William Hyll had left to the churchwardens an acre of meadow land in the Inner Marsh, which he held copyhold from the manor of Low Hall. The rent arising from this land was to be used for the expenses of a Requiem Mass on the anniversary of his death and also on the anniversaries of his mother and father.[5] The earliest surviving churchwardens' accounts in 1709 show an annual income of £1 from this land.[6] Although it is not strictly a charity for the poor, after the Reformation the churchwardens did use the income at their discretion, and the Charity of the Rev. William Hyll eventually came to be considered part of the charitable benefactions of the parish. In 1500, however, poor relief from this quarter was unlikely. The story of caring for the poor in Walthamstow had yet to begin.

One

George Monoux:
Gentleman and Benefactor

WALTHAMSTOW'S FIRST BENEFACTOR, George Monoux, was perhaps its most wealthy and most famous. Monoux began his rise to fame and fortune as a merchant adventurer in Bristol during the 1480s, exporting cloth to Bordeaux, Spain and Portugal, and importing wine, oil, salt, and sugar. Early in the 16th century he moved to London, where he continued to prosper in the cloth trade. Admitted to the freedom of the City as a member of the Drapers' Company in 1503, he served as warden of the Drapers' Company in 1505-6 and six times as master in 1508-9, 1516-17, 1520-1, 1526-7, 1532-3 and 1539-40. Having served as bailiff of Bristol in 1490-1 and mayor in 1501-2, Monoux entered the world of London politics as alderman for Bassishaw ward on 14 January 1507. By 1524 he was the City's senior alderman and continued to serve until 1541. During 1509-10 he served as sheriff of London and as lord mayor in 1514-15. In 1523 he represented the City in Parliament and was again elected mayor that year, although he declined to serve on grounds of ill health. Investing extensively in London property during his mercantile career, Monoux also acquired land in Bedfordshire, Essex, Norfolk, Yorkshire, and six other counties, including his country seat in Walthamstow, known as 'Moones', where he lived until his death on 8 February 1544.[1]

As a long-time member and master of the Drapers' Company, Monoux would have been steeped in the corporate social welfare tradition of the London livery companies.[2] Most of the livery companies provided weekly doles or annual pensions for members who, because of age or sickness or disability, could not pursue their occupations. Wealthy companymen often bequeathed money or property to establish almshouses for poor and aged companymen. On court days casual relief or almsgiving was also distributed to people who came to the livery halls to plead for charity. The Drapers, for example, 'gave a pound "for some charity and relief" to John Farrold, "being sick and his senses taken away and his wife blind"', and again, 'Stephen Malin prevailed upon the Drapers to give him a pound "towards the healing of his wife's leg broken the last great frost through a fall she had"'.[3] Such occasional assistance provided by the livery companies extended not only to their members but also to the widows and orphans of companymen. In 1567, for example, 'the Drapers gave £1 to Elizabeth, the wife of John Mitchell, "in consideration of her being great with child and her husband gone away"'.[4]

This corporate tradition of social welfare among the London livery companies also inspired and fostered a tradition of individual acts of charity among the London mercantile élite. William Jordan, in *The Charities of London 1480-1660*, calculates that during the Tudor and Stuart years 7,391 London donors gave charitable benefactions amounting to £1,889,211 12s. for relief of the poor, social rehabilitation, municipal betterments, education, and religion.[5] Over half of that total—£1,067,883 6s.—was given not by royalty, nobility, gentry, clergy or professionals, but by 2,239 London merchants, and almost all of that amount—£907,623 3s.—came from just 438 merchant adventurers and wholesalers, the commercial aristocracy of the City.[6] 'These men', comments Jordan, 'were the mercantile élite of the city. Roughly 40 per cent of their number were former lord mayors of London; another 43 per cent had been master of their livery companies or had served as sheriffs; while all the remainder were traders of great wealth and of high standing in a closely knit, highly articulate, and now confident society.'[7]

This closely knit class of men, bound together by numerous business and social ties, also shared a common world view and common aspirations at the beginning of the English Renaissance. Together they provided the leadership for the social reformation and cultural enlightenment that spread throughout the realm, relieving poverty by establishing almshouses, workhouses or apprentice foundations, and furthering education by establishing schools, lectureships and scholarships. Their endowments averaged £2072 3s. 11d. each, 'an amount quite sufficient to found a richly endowed school, to establish a great almshouse, to endow a lectureship which would in a generation re-mould the social and religious thinking of an entire community, or to care for the normal needs of the poor in an average parish'.[8] Many of these great merchants had come to London from other parts of the country and, while establishing their careers in the City, had maintained their connections with their home towns. As a result, a considerable portion of the charitable giving by London donors, amounting to £522,475 13s. or almost 28 per cent of the total benefactions during this period, went to locations outside of London. Altogether these merchant benefactors expended £82,248 in building and endowing 72 almshouses and £199,049 4s. in founding 123 endowed schools in all parts of the country.[9] Numbered among this small, but wealthy and influential, group of merchant benefactors who used their influence and money to further the social and cultural enlightenment of the English Renaissance was George Monoux, founder of the Sir George Monoux Almshouses and the Sir George Monoux School in Walthamstow.[10]

Walthamstow benefited in numerous ways from the benefactions of George Monoux. He constructed a causeway over Walthamstow Marsh and two bridges on

Lea Bridge Road. He laid earthenware pipes from Mill Field to Chapel End, supplying spring water to the entire district as well as to his house in Moones Lane, now Billet Road. In the parish church of St Mary's he repaired the north aisle and built the tower at the west end and the Monoux Chapel at the east end, where he lies buried.[11] Although his stone altar monument has disappeared from the Monoux Chapel, the school and the almshouses founded in the 16th century and still functioning today as the Sir George Monoux College and the Sir George Monoux Almshouses form his lasting monument in Walthamstow.

1 Plaque on the site of the country house of George Monoux on Billet Lane.

The original school and almshouses were designed and built to Monoux's own specification. A memorandum in George Monoux's ledger book notes that on Sunday, 16 June 1527, in the presence of witnesses his attorney Richard Vaughan took possession of the almshouse land from Prior Nicholas and the Convent of Holy Trinity Priory in Aldgate, London, with the consent of Thomas Hynchman, Vicar of St Mary's Church.[12] Rectangular in shape and situated on the north side of the churchyard, the land extended 192 feet eastward from the north gate of the churchyard and measured 40 feet wide at the east end and 34 feet wide at the west and in the middle. The memorandum then goes on to detail Monoux's design for the almshouses: 13 rooms, measuring 13 feet by 17 feet, each room having two windows, two doors, a fireplace sharing a chimney with the adjoining room, and a back yard. Forming a gabled crossing in the centre with six rooms to the west and seven to the east, would stand the schoolmaster's house, measuring 15 feet by 17 feet, with two rooms below and two above. The remainder of the 192 feet would be devoted to the party walls and gabled ends on the east and west. A pair of stairways would ascend to the long galleries on the first floor on either side of the schoolmaster's house which would be used as a schoolroom and a church house. Later documents reveal that Monoux intended that these upper rooms should be used for parish dinners and wedding feasts for poor people in the parish, a house belonging to Monoux and adjoining the almshouse property on the north having been fitted out with 'great Spitts, Andirons, Pewter, and other necessaries fitt for the dressing of the said Dinner'.[13] The memorandum concludes with Monoux's intention to provide an endowment for the repair and maintenance of the building: 'all which premisses I will shalbe alwaye for euer well ordered ruled vpholden repaired susteigned and kepte by myn Executours & ffeoffes of my last Wyll and testament concerning my landes in london'. A sketch accompanying the memorandum, presumably drawn by Monoux himself, shows the steep tiled roof of the almshouses and the gabled ends of the schoolmaster's house.

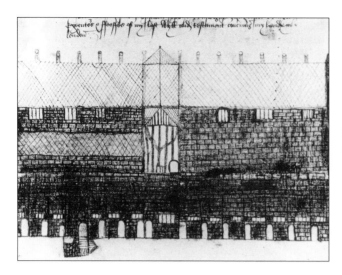

2 A sketch of almshouses in the ledger of George Monoux.

Accompanying the memorandum and sketch, but dated 1541, are the rules carefully designed by George Monoux to ensure the good governance of the almspeople and the almspriest, who would serve both as schoolmaster and as priest to the almspeople:[14]

Rules and Ordinances made by me, George Monoux, Citizen and late Lord Mayor and Alderman of the City of London, to be firmly and duly kept, observed and performed by the almspriest and schoolmaster within the cross edification and building of the almshouse by me recently built on the northside of the churchyard of the parish church of our Blessed Lady the Virgin St Mary of the parish of Walthamstow in the County of Essex within the Diocese of London.

1. First the almspriest and schoolmaster shall be quiet and of honest conversation and behaviour both in words and in deeds among the almsmen and women there for the time being and among all of the other king's loyal people.

2. And the almspriest and schoolmaster shall daily pray for the souls of me, the said George Monoux, Dame Anne Monoux, Joan Monoux my late wife, and Robert Watts, late husband of Dame Anne Monoux, and for the souls of all Christians; And upon the Sundays and holy days he shall help the vicar and curate to sing and say service from time to time in the choir of the parish church of Walthamstow.

3. And the same schoolmaster without taking of any payment or benefit more than his wages of £6 13s. 4d., paid yearly to him by me the said George Monoux or my executors and assigns, shall duly teach the children of the said parish up to the number of twenty or thirty, but not above that number except at his own will and pleasure.

4. And whereas the parish clerk there has of my gift 6s. 8d. toward his living paid yearly to him by me the said George Monoux or by my executors or assigns, he shall from time to time help to teach the said children there for the time being. And the same clerk, being unmarried, shall have a free chamber within the said cross edification of the said almshouse to be appointed by the discretion of my said executors or assigns.

5. And also the said almspriest and schoolmaster shall not absent himself from the said lodging and schoolhouse more than two days together without a special license from me the said George Monoux or from my executors or assigns.

6. And also the said schoolmaster shall once every quarter of the year teach the said almsfolk to observe and keep the rules and ordinances applicable to the alms-people.

7. And also if the schoolmaster there shall chance to be of evil conversation and negligent in teaching of the children, and if he is warned twice, but does not amend and instead offends again, then the same schoolmaster at the third offence shall be utterly dismissed from the said almshouse and school house and the whole benefit of the same: and another of good behaviour shall be placed in the said lodging and school house by my said executors or assigns.

8. And also the schoolmaster shall see the thirteen poor almsfolk well and truly paid weekly, each of them seven pence.

9. And also the schoolmaster and the thirteen poor almsmen and women shall have yearly as much coal as may be bought for £5 of good and lawful money of England by my executors or assigns, to be divided and parted equally among them yearly forever, that is, in the beginning of every month of November, December, January and February as much coal as may be provided and bought for twenty-five shillings.

Hereafter do follow and ensue the constitutions, rules and ordinances made and ordained by me George Monoux, Citizen and late Lord Mayor and Alderman of the City of London, founder of the Almshouse by me edified and builded within the Churchyard of the parish church of our Blessed Lady of Walthamstow in the County of Essex, which I will shall be firmly, duly, and truly observed and kept by the thirteen poor almsfolks, whereof eight of them always to be men, and five women that now be, and that hereafter shall be from time to time, admitted into the said Almshouse.

1. First when any man or woman shall be admitted into the said almshouse he or she shall within the parish church, kneeling before the Crucifix, devoutly say in honour of the five principal wounds of our Lord Jesus Christ, five Pater Nosters, five Aves, and a Creed; desiring in the honour of the said wounds of our Lord to be admitted into the said Almshouse. And so then immediately the same person or persons so desiring shall be freely admitted by my executors or assigns into the same. And every day afterwards at their uprising each of them shall say five Pater Nosters, five Aves, and a Creed in the honour of the five principal wounds as aforesaid.

2. And also that they and every one of them shall devoutly hear Mass daily within the said church, unless they have a lawful impediment or reasonable excuse to the contrary.

3. And also that none of the said almsfolks shall absent themselves any night, or lie out of the said almshouse without licence or reasonable cause; nor lodge, nor keep any stranger or other person within the said almshouse by night nor yet privily or secretly by day.

4. Also that every one of them be of good behaviour and keep honest rule amongst all the king's liege people there, and especially that none of them fight nor brawl amongst

themselves upon pain of expulsion out of the said almshouse. And also that every one of the almsfolk shall go to Confession quarterly, four times every year, thereby to amend their lives.

5. And also that every one of the said almsfolks shall be present in proper person at the annual memorial which shall be kept at the said parish church called the Monoux obituary, there to pray for the souls of the said founder, Dame Anne Monoux, Robert Watts her late husband, and Joan Monoux my late wife, and for all Christian souls.

6. Also if any of the said almsmen having a wife happen to outlive her, he shall no more marry upon pain of losing his room and the whole benefit thereof. And likewise every woman having a husband there and happen to outlive him, she shall no more marry upon pain of losing her room in the said almshouse with the whole benefit thereof.

7. Also if any man that now is, or hereafter shall be admitted as, one of the number of the eight almsmen having his wife with him there shall happen to die, then his wife shall be immediately discharged. In like manner, if a woman, who has been admitted as one of the number of five along with her husband, shall happen to die, then her husband outliving her shall be immediately discharged from the said almshouse and the benefit thereof.

8. Also that none of the almsfolks shall keep any person being sick of the pestilence or plague.

9. Also if any of them do misorder themselves, whereby infamy do arise, then the same thereof is to have admonition given him by my executors on two occasions; and if he do not amend his or her fault, then at the third time the same person so misordering himself is to be put out of the almshouses forever.

10. And if any of the almsfolks lay or cast anything in the churchyard that may be a nuisance to any person, or if they break any man's hedge or woods, or if any of them do frequent or sit drinking in any alehouse, and having been by my executors warned of the same on two occasions, then at the third time of offending they shall be exiled from the almshouse and the benefit thereof forever.

11. And when any of the said almsmen or women shall happen to die, then the money arising from all such vacancies shall be employed toward the repair and maintenance of the chapel and the almshouse.

As well as devising rules for the good governance of the almspeople and the schoolmaster, George Monoux also provided for the financial future of the almshouses and school in his Will, dated 6 June 1541 and proved three years later on 28 March 1544.[15] Both Thomas and George, the sons of George Monoux by his first wife Joan, had died before him; so George Monoux turned to fellow members of the Drapers' Company, Gyles Bragg and Robert Alford, to act as trustees along with Edward Broke, gentleman of Walthamstow, his kinsman Richard Monoux of Berkhamsted, his attorney Richard Vaughan, and his grandson William Monoux. To these six trustees Monoux entrusted certain lands and rents in the parish of All Hallows Stainings in the City of London amounting to a yearly value of £50 and directed that the trustees keep the premises in repair and pay yearly a sum amounting to £42 17s. 4d. toward the running costs of the almshouses and school in Walthamstow; £6 13s. 4d. annually

3 Exterior of the Sir George Monoux Almshouses and School.

to the almspriest and schoolmaster, £1 6s. 8d. quarterly to the parish clerk to help with the school, a penny a day to each of the thirteen almspeople amounting to £19 14s. 4d. annually, and £5 13s. 4d. for a Requiem Mass to be said annually in the parish church on 9 February, the day of his decease. Each year the trustees were charged to come to Walthamstow for the Requiem Mass, on pain of forfeiting for every absence ten shillings toward the repair of the almshouses. At that time they were to review the governance of the school and almshouses, making sure that all stipends were paid, that the schoolmaster and parish clerk were carrying out their duties, and that the almspeople were behaving themselves. They were further charged with the responsibility of keeping the buildings in good repair and with the responsibility of dismissing unsuitable almspeople and appointing new almspeople as vacancies occurred. When a trustee died, his trusteeship would pass to his heirs and from heir to heir forever. If the trustees failed to act, Monoux directed that the profits of his London lands and the responsibility for governing the almshouses and school should pass to his heir William Monoux; if William Monoux or his heirs failed to act, then the rents and responsibilities would pass to the Mayor and Commonalty of the City of London; and if the Corporation failed to act, then the rents and responsibilities would pass to his next male heir. In this way George Monoux sought to guarantee the perpetual maintenance of the school and almshouses and the permanent provision of education for the children and housing for the elderly poor of Walthamstow forever.

For more than two centuries following the death of George Monoux, only glimpses of the almshouses and school appear from time to time in the records. The first

4 Exterior of the Sir George Monoux Almshouses.

5 Interior of the Sir George Monoux Almshouses.

glimpse comes during the reign of Edward VI following the survey authorised by the Chantries Act 1547 of all colleges, chapels, and chantries that maintained a priest. Commissioners for Essex certified that certain lands and tenements of George Monoux were used to support a priest who sang Mass in the parish church of Walthamstow and kept a free school and that 'one Sir John Hogeson, clerke, of the age of 40 yeres, Ande of goode vsage ande conversacion, litterate and teachithe a scole their, is now Incumbent thereof.'[16]

Three years after Monoux's death the school remained in good hands; however, another glimpse offered by 17th-century court proceedings reveals that the carefully laid plans of George Monoux had begun to unravel soon thereafter.[17] His heir William Monoux had died without issue on 29 December 1549, and by 1561 all the original trustees had died or ceased to act, except the attorney Richard Vaughan, who was then in possession of the 40 tenements in London. Vaughan had also gained possession of the house adjoining the almshouse property on the north, which had been used during Monoux's lifetime as the kitchen for public feasts, for wedding dinners for poor people, and for other parish meetings held in the upper rooms of the almshouses. He had appropriated the house for his own use, pulled down some of the outbuildings on the almshouse property, and attempted unsuccessfully to convert the almshouses into a stable. In 1563 George Monoux, brother and heir of William Monoux, evicted Richard Vaughan from the London tenements, and granted possession to Edward Alford, son and heir of Robert Alford, one of the original trustees. By 1569 Edward Alford had purchased from the heirs of the other trustees all their interest in the London tenements 'upon trust that he should perform the purposes and declarations in the Will of the said Sir George Monoux'; and after Edward's death the title to the London tenements passed to his son John. Neither Edward Alford nor John Alford did 'perform the purposes and declarations in the Will of the said Sir George Monoux,' and in November

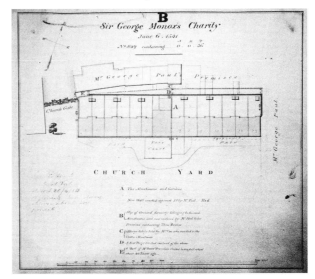

6 Nineteenth-century plan of the Sir George Monoux Almshouses.

7   Brasses of George
Monoux and Anne his wife in
St Mary's Church.

1634 the Mayor and Commonalty of the City of London, in accordance with the provisions of Monoux's Will, belatedly attempted to prove breach of trust against John Alford. The High Court of Chancery convened a Commission under the provisions of An Act to Redresse the Misimployment of Lands Goods and Stockes of Money heretofore given to Charitable Uses (43 Elizabeth), otherwise known as the Statute of Charitable Uses 1601, which took evidence at an inquisition held at Stratford Langthorne on 4 August 1635.

The commissioners reported 'that the said Edward Alford and John Alford have and do pretend to be patrons of the said Almshouse and Schoolhouse and to have the placeing and displaceing of the said Schoolmaster and poore people from tyme to tyme as their place have and shall become voide.' The commissioners went on to report that the schoolmaster, parish clerk, and almspeople 'have sometymes but not alwaies' received their stipends; that not all of the coal money had been spent; that the £5 13s. 4d. for the annual Monoux Requiem Mass had never been paid, even when the vicar had offered to preach a commemoration sermon; that the rents of the tenements in London were now worth £160 yearly, nevertheless, the schoolhouse and almeshouses and chapel 'for the space of these Twenty yeares last past have beene much ruined and in greate decay for want of necessary repaires' and that either £250 ought to be spent to put them in repair or else the almshouses should be torn down and 'new built according to the ffashion of building of Almeshouses at this day'. The list of abuses went on. Some of the schoolmasters 'have beene unfitt and not able to teach the Lattine tongue'. Edward Alford or his servants and retainers had accepted bribes to prefer people to vacant places in the almshouses. Ignoring the poor people of Walthamstow, Alford had 'placed divers poore people dwelling in remote counties and parishes to dwell in the said Almeshouse' including one 'Lunaticke person and dangerous and fearefull to divers of the Inhabitants of the said parish.' Because the stipends to the almspeople of one penny per day had not been increased in line with the rising cost of living, the parishioners of Walthamstow had been forced at their own cost not only to relieve the poverty of the almspeople through parish poor rates, but also to relieve the poverty of Walthamstow residents who should have had places in the almshouses.

At the insistence of Elizabeth Alford, mother of Edward and widow of Robert Alford, Edward Alford, 'touch'd perhaps in conscience on the point of the improved Rents',[18] in 1599 had conveyed to Thomas Colby, the schoolmaster of Walthamstow, an additional annual rent charge on the London tenements amounting to £9 to be laid out in clothing and money and food for the almspeople, but even that charity had been mismanaged and the money not always delivered.

On 18 August 1635 the Commission found John Alford guilty of breach of trust and ordered him to yield up the premises in the parish of Allhallows Stainings to the Corporation of London and to pay £500 for repair of the almshouses. Out of the rents arising from the premises in Allhallows Staynings, the Corporation was directed to increase the stipends to the schoolmaster and almspeople and to put the buildings into repair. Alford contested the commission's order in the High Court of Chancery, where the case was heard on 9 February 1637 and ultimately referred to the King's Bench. When the case was finally heard during Hilary Term in 1642, the justices found on a technicality for John Alford and against the City of London, because the City had not intervened within five years of the first breach of trust. John Alford remained in possession of the lucrative London rents, and the almspeople and schoolmaster of Walthamstow struggled to survive on their increasingly devalued stipends.[19]

By the 1650s the rents of the London properties had increased to a yearly value of over £600. The churchwardens of Walthamstow exhibited a Bill of Complaint in the Court of Chancery in 1650, but the Bill was dismissed. In 1655 the churchwardens tried again, this time raising the questions of whether the trustees and their heirs should profit personally from the increased rents and whether the almspeople in equity ought not to have their stipends increased in proportion to the increased rents. Another Commission according to the Statute of Charitable Uses, 1601 was convened, and an inquisition was held at Leytonstone on 24 March 1659. This time the Commission decreed that the heirs of Robert Alford should increase their annual payment to £115 18s. 4d., raising the schoolmaster's stipend from £6 13s. 4d. to £20 yearly, the parish clerk's stipend from £1 6s. 8d. to £3 6s. 8d., the almspeople's weekly stipend from 7d. each to 2s. each, and the ration of coal from £5 to £20 yearly.[20] Although this verdict was decided in the churchwardens' favour, it appears never to have been acted upon by the heirs of Robert Alford.

After these legal proceedings the almshouses and school largely disappear from the records until the reformation of the almshouse administration in 1782. A dispute about the northern boundary of the almshouse property was settled at a Court Baron held for the Manor of Walthamstow on 16 July 1712, and from time to time the churchwardens and Vestry put forward recommendations to the heirs of Robert Alford for filling vacancies in the almshouses.[21] Apart from these occasional glimpses, however, the Sir George Monoux Almshouses continued quietly year after year to house the elderly poor and the Sir George Monoux School continued to educate the children of Walthamstow according to the plan established by the Will of George Monoux in 1541.

Two

The Parish Poor Law System

EVEN AS GEORGE MONOUX BUILT HIS ALMSHOUSES for the elderly poor people of Walthamstow and made preparations for their perpetual maintenance, the government of Henry VIII passed in 1531 the first of a series of Tudor statutes relating to provision for the poor that would culminate in the Elizabethan Poor Law of 1601. The 1531 statute (22 Henry VIII c.12), entitled 'How Aged Poor and Impotent Persons compelled to live by alms shall be ordered', directed justices of the peace to give the impotent poor licences to beg within a defined district. In 1536 a second statute (27 Henry VIII c. 24) ordered that 'the mayor, bailiffs, constables and other head officers of cities, towns and parishes should "succour, find and keep all and every the same poor people", in such wise "as none of them of very necessity shall be compelled to wander idly and go openly in begging to ask alms".'[1] As the English Reformation gathered pace during the 1530s, bringing the dissolution of the monasteries that throughout the Middle Ages had freely distributed alms and bread to poor travellers, the need to prevent the poor from wandering from town to town and begging for food and shelter increased. These early Tudor laws, designed to control the poor and to prevent vagrancy and mendicancy, viewed poverty primarily as a problem of social disorder.

Later Tudor statutes, however, took a more balanced approach. At the heart of later Tudor legislation lay the principle of local provision for poor relief, a principle established as early as 1523 by Luther, Zwingli and other Reformers on the continent, who had argued against the indiscriminate giving of alms to the poor and for the relief of poverty by parish officers who knew the identity and problems of the poor in each locality.[2] In 1547 the Common Council in London resolved that Sunday collections in churches be abandoned and that citizens and inhabitants be assessed for a poor rate in each parish. This was followed in 1555 by the establishment of a house of correction at Bridewell for setting to work vagrants and idle persons and for harbouring the poor, the sick and the weak. A 1563 statute (5 Elizabeth c.3) ordered compulsory contributions of householders to poor relief, and a 1572 statute (14 Elizabeth c.5) directed justices of the peace to register 'aged poor, impotent and decayed persons' born within

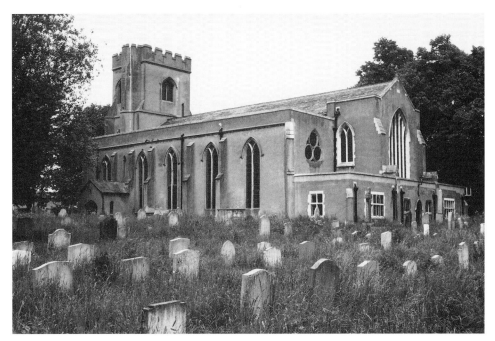

8   St Mary's Church and the churchyard.

each division of the county or who had
resided there for three years and to assess
and tax inhabitants for poor rates. Finally,
a 1576 statute (18 Elizabeth c.3) directed
parishes to provide work for the poor in
order to prevent begging. These statutes
of 1572 and 1576 extended to all 15,000
parishes and townships of the country
an embryonic Poor Law that was further
codified and elaborated in the important
statutes of 1597 and 1601.[3]

The 1597 statutes illustrate the three-
pronged attack on poverty by Elizabeth's
government. 'An Act for Punishment of
Rogues, Vagabonds and Sturdy Beggars'
(39 Elizabeth c.4) sought to discourage
exploitation of poor relief by ordering
justices of the peace to erect houses of
correction and by specifying penal measures against idlers and the able-bodied
poor who refused to earn their living. At
the same time 'An Act for erecting of
Hospitals, or Abiding and Working

Houses for the Poor.' (39 Elizabeth, c.5) encouraged the voluntary establishment of 'Hospitals, Maisons de Dieu, Abiding-places or Houses of Correction' with the twin objectives 'as well for the Finding, Sustentation and Relief of the maimed, poor, needy or impotent People, as to set the Poor to work.' The Act granted such institutions the power to be incorporated by deed enrolled in High Court of Chancery without the necessity of seeking Letters Patent under the great seal, to hold endowments to the annual value of £200 above expenses, to have a common seal, to appoint and replace staff and inmates, to buy and sell property, and so to continue forever.[4]

By far the most significant and far reaching of the three 1597 statutes, for the poor of Walthamstow and every other parish in England and Wales, was 'An act for the Relief of the Poor' (39 Elizabeth c.3).[5] This statute, revised and re-enacted in the 1601 statute (43 Elizabeth c.2) bearing the same title, created the basic system of parish poor relief that continued in force for the next two and a half centuries. The statute required the appointment in every parish of two or more overseers of the poor. Together with the churchwardens of the parish, the overseers of the poor were charged with caring for all classes of the poor and destitute residing in each parish: 'for setting to work the Children' whose parents could not maintain and keep them and 'for setting to work all such Persons, married or unmarried, having no Means to maintain them, and use no ordinary and daily Trade of Life to get their Living by'. The overseers were authorised to raise by taxation of every resident of the parish such sums of money as required to provide 'a convenient Stock of Flax, Hemp, Wool, Thread, Iron, and other necessary Ware and Stuff, to set the Poor on Work' or 'for the putting out of such Children to be Apprentices'. They were also authorised to raise 'competent Sums of Money for and towards the necessary Relief of the Lame, Impotent, Old, Blind, and such other among them, being Poor, and not able to work.' Wherever possible, parents were made legally liable to maintain their children and grandchildren, and children were made liable for their parents and grandparents, if they were unable to work. Justices of the peace were given enforcement powers to send to the house of correction anyone refusing to work or anyone refusing to pay the poor rates. Thus were established two of the three basic principles of the poor relief system: parish officers in every parish were responsible for the care of the poor in their parish, and all parishioners who owned property were obliged to pay poor rates in order to provide that care.

Following the enactment of these statutes during the 1597 session of Parliament, the Essex justices of the peace assembled for the quarter sessions at Chelmsford in April 1598 and agreed certain 'Orders vpon bothe the lawes of the Releife of ye poore and punnishment of Roages & Vagabonds.'[6] Overseers of the poor, if not already chosen for each parish, were to be named by the justices of the peace, 'the Choice to be made of the moste discreete and principall persons'. No persons except rogues and vagabonds were to be removed to their place of birth, including children under seven years of age and women with illegitimate children, but rather all were to be relieved in their parish of residence. A general house of correction for rogues and vagabonds was to be established at Coxall to serve the entire county. Particular houses of correction were to be established for each hundred, or division of the county, and justices of the peace were to appoint overseers for each house. For the Becontree Hundred, comprising the parishes of Walthamstow, Woodford, Leyton, Wanstead, West Ham, East Ham, Little Ilford, Barking and Dagenham, the house of correction was to be in Barking. In every parish Overseers were authorised to levy a poor rate of three half-pence in the pound. Finally, the justices reiterated the responsibility for each family, in the first instance, to provide poor relief: 'great grandfather grandfather father & sonne vpward & downeward in lyneall discent or degree shall releive one another as occasion shall require.'

Later in the 17th-century a further statute, entitled 'An Act for the better Relief of the Poor of this Kingdom' (13 and 14 Charles II c.12), otherwise known as the Law of Settlement and Removal, established the third important principle of parochial poor relief: every poor person had a legal settlement in one parish.[7] The 1601 statute had provided for the relief of the poor in the parish where they were residing. As the preamble of the 1662 statute makes clear,

9 Order for the Removal of Joseph Wheeler and Elizabeth his wife from Walthamstow to Stoke Newington, 19 November 1825.

however, the old problem of the poor wandering from town to town and begging for food and shelter still plagued the parochial relief system established by the earlier statute:

> by reason of some Defects in the Law, poor People are not restrained from going from one Parish to another, and therefore do endeavour to settle themselves in those Parishes where there is the best Stock, the largest Commons or Wastes to build Cottages, and the most Woods for them to burn and destroy, and when they have consumed it, then to another Parish, and at last become Rogues and Vagabonds, to the great Discouragement of Parishes to provide Stocks, where it is liable to be devoured by Strangers.

To reform this abuse of the system, the 1662 statute established the principle that every person had a settlement in one parish gained either by birth in the parish, if the child were illegitimate; by having a father legally settled in the parish; by marrying a husband in the parish; by being hired on contract as a servant for one year; by being apprenticed in the parish; or by hiring a house worth a yearly rental of at least £10. If a poor person through one or more of these means had established a legal settlement in a parish, then the parish was obliged to provide poor relief for that person. On the other hand, parish officers were empowered to apply to the justices of the peace for a warrant to remove from the parish any poor person who did not have legal settlement in that parish. Those evicted were then transported from parish to parish until they had returned to the parish where they did have legal settlement. Poor labourers were allowed to go to another parish to look for work, but only if they had a certificate from their home parish indemnifying the parish into which they went to find work. Various other clauses in the statute provided for apprehending, punishing, and transporting 'to any of the English Plantations beyond the Seas' all Rogues, Vagabonds, and Sturdy Beggars 'as shall be duly convicted and adjudged to be incorrigible'.

The law was intended to discourage vagrant beggars by requiring that any person destitute, sick, or unable to work had to be cared for by the parish where he was legally settled. Where this system of parochial provision for the poor worked well, personal acquaintance did produce compassion and sympathy. Overseers of the poor were often generous in their paternalistic concern. In many cases, however, rather than protecting the poor, the statute limited the civil liberties of the poor, for any person not belonging to the wealthy class of property owners (less than 10 per cent of the population owned or rented property with an annual value of over £10) could be summarily removed in custody and returned to his parish of legal settlement, even if he were gainfully employed and even if he had not applied for poor relief. To avoid adding poor people to the relief roll, parishes drove out the old, the poor, and the sick, wherever possible, to be resettled in some other parish. This led to litigation between parishes and attempts by churchwardens and overseers of the poor at all costs to prevent settlement in their parishes by transporting pregnant unmarried women to other parishes, by apprenticing orphan children to craftsmen in other parishes, or by limiting employment contracts to one year less one day, Lady Day being the traditional time for labourers to negotiate new contracts of employment for the following year.

How these statutes establishing the system of parochial poor relief affected Walthamstow during the 16th and 17th centuries is difficult to determine, for few of the Walthamstow parish records have survived for this period. In 1631, however, the Privy Council established a Commission for inquiring into the execution of laws for relief of the poor.[8] Justices of the peace were ordered to account to sheriffs, sheriffs to circuit judges, and judges to the Commission concerning the number of poor people given relief in each hundred. On 26 July 1636 justices of the peace filed their return for the Hundreds of Chafford, Barstable, and Becontree, reporting 48 'Poore Children put forth to Apprenticye' and 87 people 'Punnished & past away as vagarantes accordinge to the statute'.[9] There were 55 parishes in the Hundreds of Chafford, Barstable, and Becontree, including Walthamstow, suggesting an average of one poor child apprenticed in each parish and between one and two rogues and vagabonds sent from each parish to the house of correction at Coxall.

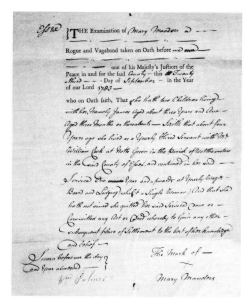
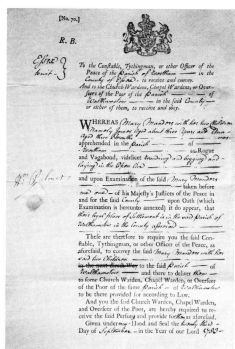

10 Examination and Order for the Removal of Mary Manders and her two children from West Ham to Walthamstow, 23 September 1783.

More firm evidence of the extent of parochial poor relief in Walthamstow comes from the earliest surviving Walthamstow Vestry minute book in the early 18th century. In April 1710, for example, James Mathews and John Acheson, overseers of the poor, were paying stipends or pensions to 20 poor people, amounting to a monthly total of £6 16s.[9] By October 1725 the pension list had increased to 30 names, including 13 widows, six adults with children, and other single adults each receiving monthly stipends between four shillings and sixteen shillings, amounting to a monthly total of £11 6s.[11] Earlier that year, at the burial of parishioner John Conyers on 19 March 1725, when at his request the sum of £10 was distributed to the 'poor of Walthamstowe,' the list contains the names of the 13 almspeople in the Monoux almshouses and 94 'other widows or poor single persons & labourers having families.'[12]

In addition to paying weekly or monthly stipends to settled pensioners, the church-wardens and overseers of the poor made numerous one-off payments to people, both residents and strangers, pleading poverty. In 1715, for example, the churchwardens made casual payments totalling £45 11s., including 1s. to 'A stranger a woman great with Child', 2s. to 'A Sergeant & 6 Soldiers', and 19s. for 'Buriall charges on a Stranger'.[13] In 1723 the Vestry 'Ordered that Mr Jones the Overseer of the Poore use his endeavour to gett Margarett Stephenson a distracted Pauper placed in Bedlam at the Parish charge'.[14] In 1724, when the bill for casual relief totalled £57 14s., payments by the churchwardens included 2s. 6d. 'To five Naked Turkey Gally Slaves in Their way home', 5s. 3d. 'To the Widdow Bigg of Wood Stret for Nurshing & Takeing Care of

Mary Green found famished on ye Forrest', and another 7s. 3d. 'Expended about her funerall', and a total of £2 11s. 9d. 'To Nursing & provideing for Iohn Todd when Ill of ye Small Pox & maintaining him till well Enough to Remove from White Chaple to Walthamstowe with Apothecaryes Bills Britches hatt & shooes.'[15]

Although the churchwardens and overseers every year made scores of such payments for the relief of sickness and poverty, whenever possible they took steps to ensure that the parish would not be legally charged with the responsibility for poor relief. Orphans or children whose parents could not maintain them were placed as apprentices, preferably outside the parish so that they would gain a legal settlement in another parish. At a Vestry meeting held on 26 November 1710, for example, it was ordered

> that James Gibson a parish Boy be placd out apprentice to Richard Pullem of St Botolph Bishopsgate in London Citizen & Silk weaver, & that three pounds be there-upon paid to the said Richard for the said apprenticeship till the Boy be of twenty one years of age, & farther one pound when the said Richard Pullem shall bind the boy to him according to the rules of the City of London.[16]

On 20 May 1722 the Vestry 'Ordered that the Widdow Butt be allowed 40s. towards putting out her son Iohn an Apprentice & for clothing him';[17] and on 30 April 1742 Peter Flower, churchwarden, was allowed expenses of £12 19s. 2d. for placing as apprentices six poor children ranging in age from nine to seventeen, all to masters outside the parish.[18]

Poor labourers arriving in the parish seeking work were examined by the Vestry or by a justice of the peace and were not allowed to stay unless they had certificates from their home parish indemnifying the parish of Walthamstow against any payment of poor relief. Beginning in January 1699, the churchwardens kept a register of such poor residents of Walthamstow who held legal settlements in other parishes, and from time to time the list was updated. In 1719, for example, all poor residents of the parish were ordered to show evidence of their legal settlement and those with legal settle-ments in other parishes were required to deposit in the parish chest their certificates.[19] Another list headed 'The Names of Several Inmates who have brought Certificates from their respective parishes which are Deposited in ye parrish Chest in ye Church March ye 29: 1726' contains 88 names, the last certificate bearing the date 2 November 1735.[20] In 1739 the Vestry appointed John Lea at an annual salary of £10 to be parish beadle, charging him to

> be particularly Carefull in Inquiring Daily after all Inmates who come to Inhabit in the said parish without Certificate and Deliver a true Account thereof from time to time to the Church Warden of the said parish. And that he Cause to be apprehended all Vagrants and Sturdy Beggers wandring in and about the said parish.[21]

In order to prevent illegitimate children gaining a legal settlement, parish officers ordered unmarried pregnant women, whose legal settlement was elsewhere, to be trans-ported out of the parish. In 1715, for example, the churchwardens paid 2s. to return

'A great belly'd woman to Tottenham'.[22] In 1724, churchwarden William Rowe paid 2s. 6d. 'To Mary Swift to Clear ye parish of her Great Belly', and another 1s. 6d. to Joseph Schooling, the parish constable, 'for Dischargeing a bigg Bellyed Woman'. Sometimes the situation became urgent, as in November that year, when a total of 7s. 6d. was expended for 'Charges Concerning Sarah Watkins near Crying Out to ye Church Wardens of Waltham Abby with other Charges in Goeing severall Times after ye Church Wardens & Overseers of said Parish to persuade Them to take their Parish Girl.'[23] If an illegitimate child was born in the parish, the overseers paid for its care, while at the same time pursuing the father in order to recover their expenses. At a Vestry meeting held on 26 December 1724, for example, 'the Widdow Osborne was ordered twelve pence per weeke addition to her present Pension, for & towards the maintaining of her grand-daughter Martha the daughter of Iohn Ienkins sawyer untill the said

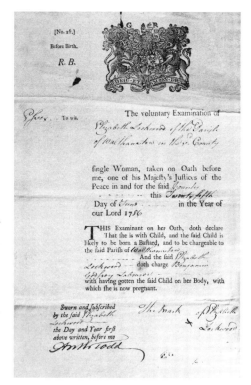

11 Bastardy Examination of Elizabeth Lockwood, 25 June 1786.

Iohn Ienkins can be found, who ought to maintaine her.'[24] In 1742, churchwarden Peter Flower recovered from Robert Warton 'Six pounds to deffray this Parish of ye Charges of a Bastard Child (Robert) begotten on the Body of francis Goodwin of this Parish haveing gained a settlement by servitude to Mr Turrell.' The unfortunate Robert Warton had been apprehended and 'had been kept at hard Labour above 2 Months in the House of Correction at Barking.'[25]

In spite of such vigilance on the part of the churchwardens and overseers of the poor, the bill for caring for the poor rose relentlessly. All property in Walthamstow was surveyed to determine its annual rental value, and property owners were assessed poor rates of so many pence per pound of rental value. From the rate of three half-pence in the pound first ordered by the Essex justices of the peace in April 1598, the poor rate in Walthamstow had increased by 1725 to three and one-half pence in the pound levied by the overseer of the poor every six months. To that annual tax burden of seven pence in the pound was added in the decade between 1716 and 1725 a churchwarden's rate averaging almost five pence in the pound for further poor relief. The tax burden would have been much higher, however, if it had not been for Walthamstow's numerous 17th-century benefactors of the poor.

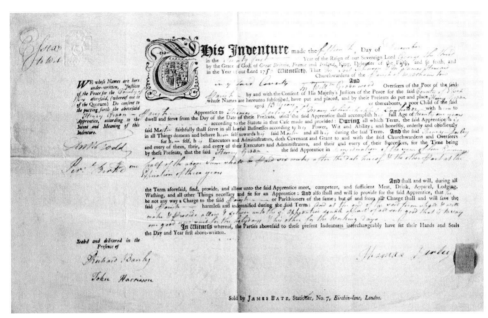

12   Apprenticeship Indenture of Henry Green, aged 13, of Walthamstow to Thomas Darley, innkeeper of St Mary Whitechappel, 15 December 1780.

13   Rate Book of John Thornell, Overseer of the Poor, Michaelmas 1742.

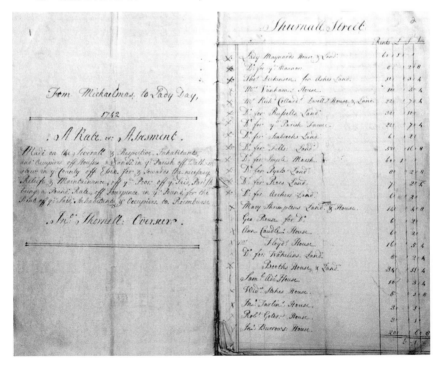

Three

The 17th-Century Charities

APART FROM THE CHARITY OF GEORGE MONOUX, augmented by the gift of Elizabeth and Edward Alford in 1599, the only other 16th-century parish charity was established in 1585 by Robert Rampston, Yeoman of the Chamber to Edward VI, Queen Mary, and Elizabeth I, and resident of the neighbouring parish of Chingford. In his Will dated 2 August 1585, Robert Rampston left the annual sum of £22 arising from the rents of his freehold lands and tenements to be paid to the poor of 12 Essex parishes, including 'to the poor of Walthamstow, yearly for ever, 40s.'[1] Commemorated by the brass tablet in the north aisle of St Mary's Church, this annual rentcharge arising from the Stone Hall Estate in Dunmow, Essex, has over the centuries been paid to the Walthamstow churchwardens. Rampston did not specify how the money was to be spent, but the records indicate that from early times it was distributed in bread.

Other Walthamstow charities were specifically created to provide weekly distribution of bread to the poor. On 20 November 1623, William Conyers, serjeant-at-law of the Middle Temple and executor of the Will of his uncle Tristram Conyers, late of Walthamstow, conveyed to the churchwardens and overseers of the poor an annuity of £7 10s. payable out of his lands in Walthamstow commonly known as Sheepcoate Breach, Middle Breach, Feather Breach, Slipe and Stakefield. With this annuity 12 threepenny loaves of bread were to be purchased each week, placed on the stone altar monument of George Monoux in the north aisle during the Sunday morning service, and distributed afterwards to 12 poor persons of the parish. The 12 poor persons, 'whether almsfolks or other poor of this parish', were to be chosen annually by the churchwardens and overseers of the poor with the consent of four other inhabitants 'to be appointed by the greater number of the better sort of the said parish'. The names of the persons appointed to receive the loaves were to be written on a parchment roll entitled 'Note of the poor Inhabitants of the parish of Walthamstow as are to receive for this year following by the number of twelve every sabbath day, Three pence in Bread by the Gift of Mr. Tristram Conyers late of Walthamstow Esqr.'[2]

Two additional bread charities were created in January 1642. In his Will proved on 6 January 1642, Richard Garnett bequeathed to the churchwardens and overseers of the poor an annuity of £3 arising from his tenements and lands on Marsh Street in Walthamstow. Beginning on the first Sunday of November, loaves of bread worth one penny or two pence each were to be distributed to the poor up to a weekly maximum expenditure of 2s. 6d. Such distribution was to continue Sunday by Sunday each year until the £3 had been used up. Later that same month in his Will dated 23 January 1642, Thomas Gamuel, a rich London grocer living in Walthamstow, bequeathed some six acres of copyhold land known as Honeybone Field and Markhouse Common to serjeant-at-law William Conyers and five other trustees. From the rents and profits of this land Gamuel directed that 12 pence a week should be laid out in penny loaves of bread to be distributed in the parish church of Walthamstow every Sunday morning by the churchwardens and overseers of the poor. The residue of the profits above this sum of £2 12s. was left to the discretion of the churchwardens and overseers to be distributed to the poor on 24 December each year.[3]

In accordance with these bequests the earliest surviving churchwardens' accounts in the year beginning Easter 1709 show payments for bread of £2 12s. from the charity of Thomas Gamuel, £3 from Richard Garnet, £7 10s. from Tristram Conyers, and £2 from Richard Rampston. Early in the 18th century three additional bread charities were established. Anthony Compton, in his Will dated 20 January 1703, gave to the vicar, churchwardens and overseers of the poor the sum of £20 to be invested for the benefit of the poor, the interest being used to purchase bread for distribution on New Year's Day. To this sum his sister Dinah Compton, in her Will dated 23 September 1706, added a further £5. Thomas Turner, in his Will dated 18 May 1711, expressed his desire to be buried in the churchyard of St Mary's, Walthamstow and bequeathed £130 to be invested for the upkeep of his gravestone and for distribution of bread to the poor each Sunday. The Compton gifts came into the possession of the church-wardens in 1708 and the Turner bequest in 1716. Together with the interest accrued, the sums were eventually invested in £180 of South Seas Annuity Stock in 1728. Altogether these charities of Turner, Compton, Gamuel, Garnett, Conyers, and Rampston yielded an annual income in the mid-18th century of £20 7s. 6d. for bread distribution. A memorandum in the Vestry minute book dated 15 July 1741 reveals that the churchwardens had contracted with John Shrimpton, a local baker, for the weekly production and distribution of 32 threepenny loaves.[4]

In addition to these bread charities, other parish charities were bequeathed generally for the poor of Walthamstow to be distributed at the discretion of the vicar or churchwardens or overseers of the poor. In 1609, Thomas Colby, schoolmaster of the Sir George Monoux School, died of the plague, leaving all of his estate to George Sohne and William Soane in trust for the use of the poor of Walthamstow. Like the trustees of George Monoux, the trustees of Thomas Colby failed to carry out their trust. A Commission convened according to the Statute of Charitable Uses held an inquisition in Walthamstow on 6 June 1633 and found that George Sohne, the surviving executor, still held £71 belonging to Colby's estate. The Court of Chancery ordered Sohne to pay the £71 to the churchwardens of Walthamstow along with an additional £50 for breach of trust. The court further directed the churchwardens to purchase land yielding a yearly rental value of £7 and to distribute the profits among the poor of the parish and the residents of the almshouse each year on St Thomas Day.[5] Accordingly, on 23 June 1635, the churchwardens purchased from George Rodney, lord of the manor of Walthamstow Toni, 'three pieces of ground at Hale End' containing about twelve acres of land, some of which is still used in the parish for allotments.[6]

A second discretionary charity, known as the Inhabitants' Donation, produced in the 17th century a further annual income of £5. Several unnamed Walthamstow parishioners had given to Tristram Conyers, Charles Maynard, Ralph Skipwith, Richard Cooper, Sigismund Trafford, William Batten, John Bassano, William Harloe, Henry Wolleston, Richard Coxe, Ralph Barker, Michael Garnett, John Shirton, William Miller, Richard Thorneton, Thomas Brooke, Richard Collard, Nicholas Harris and Toby Maynard the sum of £95 upon trust to purchase lands and tenements, the profits thereof to go to the relief of the poor of the parish at their or the churchwardens' discretion. With this money on 23 October 1650 the trustees purchased from Robert Rowe of Low Leyton 16 acres of land, pasture, and woodland, known as Winsbeach Field, 'in trust, yearly to give and dispose all the rents and profits of the said premises to and amongst the poor of the said parish, where most need should be, upon the feast day of St Thomas the Apostle for ever'.[7]

Further discretionary funds came from the bequest of Edward Corbett, citizen of London and member of the Cooks' Company. Born in Walthamstow in May 1613, Corbett had been apprenticed at parish expense. Having succeeded in his trade, he showed his gratitude in his Will dated 5 April 1674 and proved on 13 July 1676, by leaving property located on Wyatts Lane worth £10 in yearly rents and desiring the parish officers 'to bestow that his small mite as their christian wisdom should think fit'. The only instructions left by Corbett were to divide the sum as follows: £7 'to the poor of the parish of Walthamstow' and £3 'for a Sermon and Entertainment on the anniversary of his birth' comprising 20s. to the minister for the sermon, 10s. to the parish clerk, and 30s. to the churchwardens 'to be spent on a supper or dinner, which they should think fit, with the minister and whom they please'.[8]

By far the largest discretionary bequest was given by Sir Henry Maynard. Baptised in Walthamstow on 2 August 1646 and buried in St Mary's Church on 27 November 1686, Sir Henry Maynard belonged to a wealthy and distinguished Essex family, who in Sir Henry's time held the Manor of Walthamstow Toni. In his Will dated 18 November 1686, Sir Henry left extensive bequests including £100 to repair the church, £50 to repair the Sir George Monoux School, £50 for purchase of communion plate, £20 to the vicar for preaching his funeral sermon, and £10 to be distributed to the poor after his funeral. In addition to these gifts Maynard left £950 to trustees to be invested in lands in trust for the following beneficiaries: the income from £400 to the vicar, the income from £200 to the schoolmaster to be used 'in teaching and

14 The monument of Sir Henry Maynard, 1646-86, in St Mary's Church.

instructing eight poore children of Walthamstow', the income from £50 to provide annual payments of 10s. to the parish clerk and rings to the churchwardens and overseers of the poor 'for their care and pains in distributing the yearly charity by me given to the poore of the said parish', and the income from £300 to be distributed by the churchwardens and overseers of the poor each year on St Thomas Day and on the anniversary of his death 'amongst the poore and reall necessitous Inhabitants of the said parish by equall proportions in every yeare'.[9]

On 4 November 1690 William Scawen, the surviving executor of Henry Maynard, bought land on Higham Hill Road known as Bulls Farm for £1,000 and allegedly conveyed it to trustees on 1 March 1691.[10] When no income was forthcoming from this trust, a Commission convened under the Statute for Charitable Uses held an inquisition at Leytonstone on 8 June 1699 and, after hearing evidence, decreed that William Scawen should pay interest or damages amounting to £685 10s. for detaining the income of his trust since 18 November 1687.[11] Legal proceedings in the High Court of Chancery followed, with William Scawen in 1703 filing exceptions to the decree, claiming that Henry Maynard had left insufficient funds to pay his bequests and that he himself had used £250 of his own money secured by a mortgage to purchase Bulls Farm and that this transaction had taken place with the full approval of the inhabitants of the parish.[12] James Barker, vicar of Walthamstow, and Gabriel Williams and Jeremiah Wakelyn, churchwardens, filed an answer to these exceptions in 1704, claiming that Maynard had left plenty of money to pay his bequests and that no meeting of the Vestry had ever discussed Scawen's purchase.[13] The hearing eventually took place in the Court of Chancery on 30 October 1706 before the Lord Keeper, who ordered that William Scawen quit claim to his interest in the land, that the land be conveyed to new trustees appointed by the Court, and that the rents and profits arising from the land be computed by the Court and paid to the new trustees.[14] A Court Order was made in 1714 for the distribution of the rents and profits arising from Maynard's bequest, and a further Order in 1720 confirmed the purchase of additional copyhold land in Walthamstow known as Stretmans Farm with the £450 in profits of the Sir Henry Maynard Charity still remaining in the hands of the Court.[15] By 1709, the churchwardens were accounting for rents from Bulls Farm and, according to the terms of the Sir Henry Maynard

Charity, making annual payments of £20 to the vicar, £10 to the schoolmaster, £2 10s. to the parish officers, and £15 in discretionary funds for the poor.

The full effect of these parish charities established by Walthamstow benefactors during the 16th and 17th centuries may be gauged from a closer inspection of the earliest surviving accounts of the overseers of the poor and the churchwardens.[16] The overseers collected poor rates from every property owner in the parish and from the proceeds paid weekly or monthly stipends to parishioners in need. Each year at Lady Day and Michaelmas the Walthamstow Vestry approved a list of poor parishioners who would receive these pensions. The earliest overseer's records, those for the year beginning Easter 1710, include a pension list 'for relief of certain poor of this parish to continue for seven months from the 8th day of April to the 21st of October 1710'. The list contains the names of 20 people, each receiving between 4s. and 12s. monthly, such as 10s. to 'Widow Philips and one child allowd per month', or 12s. to 'R. Deaths wife till her husband comes home for herself & children', the total expenditure each month amounting to £6 16s. From time to time the Vestry added new names to the list or adjusted the pension amounts. The accounts of John Acheson, overseer of the poor during this year, show two poor rates, each of three pence in the pound, levied at Lady Day and Michaelmas and bringing in a total of £109 15s. 6d. As well as paying the monthly pensions agreed by the Vestry, Acheson also made numerous emergency or casual payments, called 'other particulars' in his accounts, whenever so ordered by the churchwardens or justices of the peace.

Accounts of Overseer of the Poor 1710-1711

Receipts	£	s.	d.
Poor Rate to October 1710	54	16	09
Poor Rate to 24 March 1711	54	18	09
Due by Balance to J. Acheson			
as Overseer	0	01	11
	109	17	05
Expenditure	£	s.	d.
Summer pension	49	07	00
Other particulars paid	9	08	00
Winter pension	48	07	06
Widow Wilden's bill	1	00	02
Other particulars amongst which			
for charges of a man drowned	7	05	00
Deficiencies in the Rate	4	10	09
	109	17	05

In addition to collecting the two threepenny poor rates this year, John Acheson was also deputised by order of the Vestry on 8 May 1710 to collect two additional threepenny rates to cover the deficit in the churchwardens' accounts for the previous

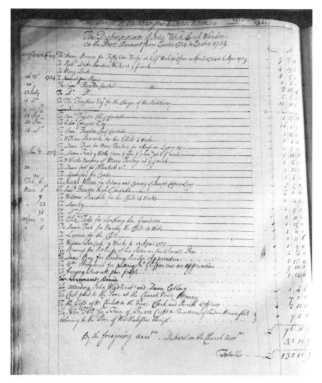

15 Disbursements to the Poor by John White, Churchwarden, April 1735.

16 Payments to Pensioners Settled in Walthamstow, October 1730.

year, making total rates of one shilling in the pound levied on Walthamstow parishioners this year. Expenditure of the churchwardens in the year beginning Easter 1709 is divided into two main headings: 'The Bill of Disbursements of ye Church account' and 'The bill of Disbursements on the poor account'. Church expenses, including payments to carpenters, stonecutters, painters, expenses of the archdeacon's visitation, Communion bread and wine, and a folio common prayer book for the reading desk, amount to £49 14s. In addition to these payments, the churchwardens also accounted for £20 paid to the vicar and £12 10s. paid to the schoolmaster and parish officers for their shares of Maynard's Charity, £1 5s. to the minister and parish clerk for their share of Edward Corbett's Charity and £1 'for the supper on Mr. Corbett's birthday', £1 10s. for the parish constable, and five guineas for the wages of the parish clerk, making total church expenses of £91 4s. for the year ending Easter 1710.

The bill of expenditure for the poor consists primarily of casual payments, such as £1 10s. for 'cloathing two children at widow Bakers', 15s. for 'clothing a child at Masons', 7s. 7d. for 'sickness & buryal of a woman that died at George Turners', 18s. for 'apprenticing a child to James Carter & charges', and a series of payments for the unfortunate Bartholomew Gutteridge including £1 to the surgeon 'for attending Barth. Gutteridge when he cut his throat', 12s. 7d. for further medical expenses 'of Bart. Gutteridge his sickness (after cutting his throat)', 1s. 6d. to 'the person who called ye surgeon', 6s. 6d. for 'going to ye coroner & summoning ye Jury', £1 10s. for the coroner's fee, and a further 9s. 6d. for the 'expences of the coroner and jury', In addition to these casual payments to the poor, amounting to £70 8s. 7d., the churchwardens also distributed a total of £15 2s. in bread from the income of the charities of Rampston, Garnett, Gamuel and Conyers. The £7 income from Colby's charity was distributed to the poor on 21 December, and the £15 income from 'the poors share' of Maynard's charity was distributed on 27 November and 21 December. Whether these sums were distributed in bread or coal or money is not specified. Altogether the churchwardens' payments to the poor this year totalled £107 10s. 7d.

Churchwardens' Expenses 1709-1710

For the use of ye Church	£	s.	d.	For ye Use of ye Poor	£	s.	d.
Corbett's gift to vicar and clerk	1	05	0	Maynard's Charity	15	00	0
Corbett's birthday supper	1	00	0	Colby's Charity	7	00	0
Maynard's gift to vicar	20	00	0	Bread Charities	15	02	0
Maynard's gift to clerk				Bill of Disbursements	70	08	7
and schoolmaster	12	10	0				
Hire of Constable	1	10	0				
Parish Clerk's wages	5	05	0				
Bill of Disbursements	49	14	0				
Total	91	04	0		107	10	7

The income to pay for these expenses of the churchwardens came primarily from two sources: parish charities and churchwardens' rates. Apart from the fine for John Barton's failure to serve as a parish officer and the small amount collected for bell ringing and burial expenses, most of the income for the church account before the rate was levied—a total of £35 5s.—came from the Rev. William Hyll's Charity and the church officers' shares of Maynard's Charity and Corbett's Charity. Income for the poor account, apart from monies received from the sale of the goods of the late William Gibson and the late unfortunate Bartholomew Gutteridge, came in the first instance from the charities of Maynard, Gamuel, Colby, Corbett, Conyers, Garnett, Rampston, and the Inhabitants' Donation, amounting to total charity income of £49 12s. out of the £54 7s. 6d. total income on the poor account. The shortfall of £43 19s. on the church account and £53 3s.1d. on the poor account was then met by two church-wardens' rates, each for threepence in the pound, levied at the end-of-year vestry meeting on 8 May 1710.

Churchwardens' Receipts for 1709-1710

For the use of ye Church	£	s.	d.	For ye Use of ye Poor	£	s.	d.
Corbett's gift to parish officers	2	05	0	Rent of Maynard's land	15	00	0
John Barton's fine	10	00	0	Residue of Gamuel's land		10	0
Maynard's gift to vicar, schoolmaster and clerk	32	00	0	Rent of Colby's land	7	00	0
Rent of Rev. Hyll's land	1	00	0	Rent of Corbett's land and the Inhabitants' Donation	12	00	0
Bell and ground	2	00	0	Conyer's Garnett's, Gamuel's, & Ramston's gifts for bread	15	02	0
Subtotal	47	05	0	the goods of Bart. Gutteridge	2	13	4
				the goods of Wm. Gibson	2	02	2
Churchwardens' Rate to balance	43	19	0	Subtotal	54	07	6
				Churchwardens' Rate to balance	53	03	1
Total	91	04	0		107	10	7

Charity income, and particularly the discretionary charity income, in effect was used by the churchwardens to subsidise the level of rates paid by the more wealthy Walthamstow residents. Out of the £49 12s. of charity income received for the poor account in 1709, only £37 2s. was distributed directly to the poor on the days specified by the donors. The remaining £12 10s., being the discretionary income from Corbett's Charity, the Inhabitants' Donation, and the residue of Thomas Gamuel's bread charity that should have been distributed on 24 December, was applied instead toward the bill for casual disbursements to the poor, thus lowering the shortfall required to be made up by the churchwardens' rates. The same policy was followed on the church account with the income from the Rev. William Hill's Charity applied to general church expenses in order to lower the shortfall to be made up by the rates. As the expense of caring

17 Vestry Minutes, 7 April 1735, Appointing Overseers of the Poor and Ordering the Payment of Casual Poor Relief.

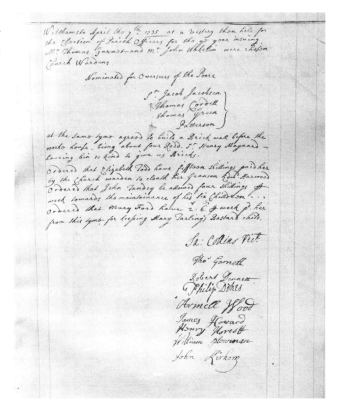

for the poor increased during the 18th century, parish officers increasingly relied on the income from charitable bequests to relieve the growing pressure on parish rates. Forty years later in 1749, for example, when the poor rate collected by the overseers had soared to an annual total of 14 pence in the pound, the churchwardens held their rate at four pence by using their discretionary charity income. Although the annual income from charity lands had increased to £132 2s. that year, only £29 15s. was distributed directly to the poor in bread and alms and £48 13s. to the vicar, school-master, and parish officers according to the wishes of the benefactors. The remaining £53 6s. of charitable income was set against the deficit in the church account and the poor account, resulting in a reduction of over twopence in the pound on the church-wardens' rate. Not even the increasing bulwark of charitable legacies, however, could protect Walthamstow parishioners from the steadily rising costs of caring for the poor; thus in 1726 the vestry voted to build a parish workhouse and set the poor to work.

Four

Setting the Poor to Work

FROM THE VERY BEGINNING the poor laws had pursued the panacea of setting the poor to work. The 1601 statute 'An Act for the Relief of the Poor' had not only ordered the overseers of the poor to set to work 'all such Persons, married or unmarried, having no Means to maintain them, and use no ordinary and daily Trade of Life to get their Living by', but had also permitted parish officers to provide through taxation or poor rates 'a convenient Stock of Flax, Hemp, Wool, Thread, Iron, and other necessary Ware and Stuff, to set the Poor on Work'.[1] It is not surprising, therefore, to discover the subject appearing in the earliest surviving Walthamstow Vestry book. The Vestry meeting on 12 November 1711, for example, ordered both 'that the Church Wardens Contrive some way for the Maintaining and Employing Parish Children till they are fitt to goe abroad' and 'that the Church Wardens buy 20 Spinning wheels with Reels for Pensioners & Parish Children'.[2] Accounts of churchwarden John Bocock for the year 1711 include expenses of £1 7s. 'at a vestry to find out a way to imploy the poor' and a further 19s. 6d. 'at another vestry to find out a way to imploy the pore'.[3] Nor is it surprising to find that within three years after Parliament approved the building of parish workhouses, Walthamstow was one of the first parishes in Essex to adopt the workhouse solution to the problem of caring for the poor.

The first general workhouse had been built in Bristol in 1697, an experiment copied by perhaps a couple of hundred other places across the nation in the early 18th century. In 1723 'An Act for amending the Laws relating to the Settlement, Imployment, and Relief of the Poor,' otherwise known as the Knatchbull Act, endorsed this development, and authorised all churchwardens and overseers of the poor

> to purchase or hire any House or Houses in the same Parish, Township or Place, and to contract with any Person or Persons for the lodging, keeping, maintaining and employing any or all such Poor in their respective Parishes, Townships or Places, as shall desire to receive Relief or Collection from the same Parish, and there to keep, maintain and employ all such poor Persons, and take the Benefit of the Work, Labour and Service of any such poor Person or Persons, who shall be kept or maintained in any such House or Houses, for the better Maintenance and Relief of such poor Person or Persons, who shall be there kept or maintained.

The statute also authorised parish officers to deny poor relief to anyone who refused to enter the parish workhouse:

> in case any poor Person or Persons of any Parish, Town, Township or Place where such House or Houses shall be so purchased or hired, shall refuse to be lodged, kept or maintained in such House or Houses, such poor Person or Persons so refusing shall be put out of the Book or Books where the Names of the Persons, who ought to receive Collection in the said Parish, Town, Township or Place, are to be registred, and shall not be entitled to ask or receive Collection or Relief from the Churchwardens and Overseers of the Poor of the same Parish, Town or Township.[4]

This provision, commonly known as 'the workhouse test' or 'the offer of the house', often deterred claims for poor relief, resulting in a marked decline in poor rates. By 1725 other Essex parishes with workhouses included Barking, Romford, Brentwood, Maldon, Colchester, and Chelmsford.[5] All testified to a drop in the poor rates.

Taking note of their success in deterring people from claiming poor relief, the Vestry agreed on 27 December 1725 to try the workhouse experiment in Walthamstow.

> Whereas ye Care & Charge of ye poor begins very sensibly to encrease with in yis our parish, and whereas ye establishing of workhouses in several parts of ye nation for entertaining maintaining & Employing therein ye poor, hath bene found highly advantagiouse to all respective parishes, as well as Comfortable to ye poor themselves. It's therefore resolved & Ordered by us now in Vestry assembled yat ye present Church-wardens & Overseers of ye poor with Certain other persons here under named bee hereby requested & Empowered to Act as a Committee of Vestry, & as such they or any five of them to treat & agree for a proper House to bee taken for three years from Lady day next, for ye reception & Employment of all such poor as shal receive or require legal maintenance of ye parish, & yat ye said house being actually hired & in possession of ye parish officers, all such persons as now receive pentions, or mony for rent, bee forthwith removed & placed by ye Overseers of ye poor in ye said house, those of ye alms house only excepted.

In addition the committee was ordered to 'draw upp a Certain Method of manageing ye said house & poor therein, & of furnishing ye same with all necessary provisions for yeir support, & also all materials & instruments necessary for setting yem to work.'[6] On 5 January the committee arranged to lease a house on Hoe Street from Joseph Schooling for three years from 25 March at £14 a year, and at a Vestry meeting on 21 March the churchwardens were ordered to 'forthwith provide ye several sorts of Household furniture'.[7] At a further Vestry meeting on 28 March, Thomas King and his wife were hired as governor and governess of the workhouse at a salary of 5s. a week; the rules and orders to be observed in the workhouse were read and agreed; and the committee was authorised to agree with the butcher, baker, brewer, and other tradesmen for supplying provisions for the workhouse.[8] By Monday, 4 April 1726, the workhouse was operational.

On the same day the Vestry voted to meet the immediate workhouse expenses by borrowing from the Charity of Sigismund Trafford, who by his Will in 1723 had left to the minister and churchwardens an annual rentcharge of £10 arising from his property in Lincolnshire known as Grange Hill Farm. Trafford had directed that 10 shillings were to be paid each year to the sexton to clean the Trafford family monument in the church, that the sum of £50 was to be accumulated for the repair and maintenance of the elaborate ironwork and marble of the monument, and that all further sums not needed for repairs were to be used at the discretion of the Vestry, minister, and churchwardens. Although only three annual payments had been received, leaving the sum of £28 10s. after subtracting the sexton's fees, the Vestry agreed to borrow the remainder for workhouse expenses and to reimburse the charity funds out of the next rate of the overseer of the poor.[9]

As the parish poor entered the workhouse during the first week of April 1726, the number of settled pensioners receiving weekly relief dropped from 30 to 7, and the payments by the overseer for this outdoor relief dropped from £11 6s. a month to

18   Monument of Sigismund Trafford, d. 1723, in St Mary's Church.

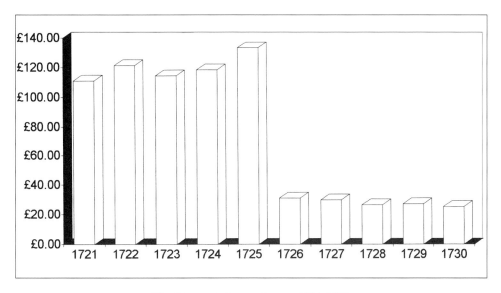

19 Payments to pensioners, 1721-1730.

£2 12s.[10] Total annual payments to settled pensioners, which had climbed to a high of £133 in 1725, dropped to £31 8s. in 1726 and to £25 7s. by the end of the decade. During the 1730s the total annual pension payments continued to fall. At first the 'offer of the house' seemed to be working so well that in 1729 the Walthamstow Vestry decided to make the workhouse permanent.

At a meeting on 26 December 1729, the Vestry agreed to purchase an acre of land and build 'a house for ye better releif & maintenance of ye poor Commonly called a Workhouse'. To finance the project, the Vestry decided unanimously to sell the £180 of South Sea Annuity stock, being the principal of the bread charities of Thomas Turner and Anthony and Dinah Compton, and agreed to raise annually by the poor rates the sum of £8, a sum equal to the annual interest arising from these charitable legacies, to be distributed weekly to the poor in bread according to the will of the donors.[11] The sale of stock raised £187 13s. 6d., to which was added on 11 May 1730 a donation of £100 from Thomas Clark in exchange for a five per cent annuity paid to him for the rest of his natural life.[12] The final accounts for purchasing the land and for building the workhouse show a total expenditure of £344 18s. 11d., paid for by the donations of Turner, Compton, and Clark, the remainder being charged to the poor rates.[13] When the workhouse was finished in 1730, on the stone lintel over the main door was carved the following inscription:

> This House Erected
> An. Dom. MDCCXXX
> if any would not work
> neither Should he eat.

The Walthamstow workhouse, in the words of Jeremy Bentham, would be 'a mill to grind rogues honest, and idle men industrious'.[14] In the workhouse the poor would earn their keep, relieving the burden on ratepayers, and in the workhouse the poor would be taught skills, discipline and piety. All birds would be killed with one elegant stone.

From the very beginning, however, it should have been clear that the poor could never pay their way. In the second year of operation, for example, workhouse accounts for a typical month—July 1727—show payments totalling £1 11s. 3d. to the butcher for 105 lb. and 4 stone of beef, 1 shin of beef, and 4 sheep's heads; £2 9s. 4d. to the baker for 52 loaves, 2 pecks of flour, and 2 pecks of oatmeal; 16s. to the brewer for 72 gallons of beer; 11s. 6d. for butter and cheese; 1s. 11½d. to the chandler for 1 pint sugar, ½ pint vinegar, ½ peck salt, tape, starch, thread, and nails; and 18s. 7d. to the governor for yarn, mending of shoes, milk, soap, carriage, cloth, aprons, and hoops. In the same month receipts for spinning, scouring, nursing, and other occasional labour by the poor amounted to only 2s. 6d. During the full year from Easter 1727 to Easter 1728 the workhouse accounts show total payments to the butcher of £17 8s. 1d., to the baker £34 15s. 1d., to the brewer £11 11s., for butter and cheese £11 5s. 8d. ob., to the chandler £1.18s. 8d., and to the workhouse governor £4 17s. 9d. ob. Altogether the Overseers of the Poor paid £109 15s. that year for workhouse expenses. Total receipts for the year are missing, but during the decade between 1735 and 1744 annual receipts for spinning of wool and silk thread by workhouse inmates and for the occasional work of able bodied men or boys averaged just £6 11s. 10d.[15]

The impossibility of profitably employing the poor in the parish workhouse is succinctly summed up by historian Roy Porter:

> As economical cures for poverty, workhouses proved duds. One problem was that the inmates were—by definition—the nation's most unpromising work-force: a rubbish tip including the very young and the aged, the chronic sick and infirm, rogues, vagrants, and village simpletons. Many were unemployed and on the parish because of trade slumps: the hope that self-financing workhouses could somehow buck the economic trend was moonshine.[16]

The Walthamstow workhouse was no exception. A record of workhouse inmates dated 16 October 1743, for example, shows a total of 32 people, mostly very young and very old, including 12 women aged 27 to 82, 3 men aged 33 to 60, 5 boys aged 1 to 16, and 12 girls aged 4 to 14.[17]

Nevertheless, parish officers still pursued the elusive goal of setting the poor to work. In February 1756 the Vestry resolved to borrow £400 in order

> to Inlarge The work House and To Furnish it with all sorts of Furniture that is wanted and to Take all the Poor In to the said work House when they become Chargeable And to allow no weekly Pention and to Take a Governor and Governess into the work House to Imploy the said Poor For the Use and Bennefit of the Parish.[18]

Ultimately, an additional rate of threepence in the pound was levied on the parish to pay for the enlargement; and during the summer of 1756 a two-storey extension, including a long workroom below and a dormitory above, was added at the back of the workhouse.[19]

On 19 March 1780 the Vestry again resolved 'that the Present Church Wardens & Overseers of the Poor be desired to make Enquiry of the best manner of Employing the Poor.'[20] When the committee appointed to inquire into the state of the poor made its report on 26 June 1780, they recommended that the men and boys in the workhouse be employed 'in cultivating the Garden for the Use of the House, Picking Oakam, Spinning Hemp or flax, & such other business as the Officers shall from time to time with the approbation of the Justices Appoint', The women and girls should be employed 'in spinning of flax for sheeting, Hemp for Sacks &c, Yarn for stockens, & Knitting the same for the use of the house, Making & Mending & Washing Linnen, Cleaning the House, & such other business as shall be directed as aforesaid'. To these recommendations the committee added the warning that all the poor should

> be made diligently to apply themselves under Pain of the severest Penalties to be inflicted by the Laws in Case of disobedience & they are not to use any abusive obscene or bad language among themselves to any Person whatever but behave Orderly and reverence their Benefactors & Governors.[21]

In 1785 William Dallet, the new governor of the workhouse, further proposed to 'employ the Poor to advantage in the winding & Preparing of Cotton to the Tallow Chandlers'.[22]

Even more than a century after the construction of the workhouse, the Workhouse Management Committee in 1831 was still attempting unsuccessfully to set the poor to work. After a visit to the workhouse on 14 November 1831, the committee reported:

> They regret to state that with the exception of those occupied in the domestic concerns of the House, the inmates are totally unemployed, though many of them are capable of performing any work of a light description. They therefore recommend that a quantity of Yarn be provided for the employment of the children in Knitting under the direction of one of the female inmates, and that the House be by these means supplied with Stockings. They also recommend that a quantity of Flannel and linen be purchased, and that all the females, be employed in making these into such articles of Clothing and bedding, as may be required in the House from time to time, and by the Overseers to Supply the necessities of the out door poor. They further recommend that whenever the children can be employed in usefull work in the House, that they attend the National School for the purpose of Religious instructions only.[23]

The persistence with which the Walthamstow Vestry pursued the notion of setting the poor to work can in part be explained by the inexorable rise in the cost of caring

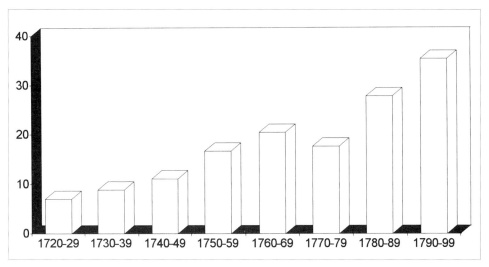

20   Average poor rate by decade, 1720-1780

for the poor throughout the 18th century. In 1711, the earliest surviving overseer's accounts show a total annual poor rate of 6d. in the pound. By 1800, however, the total poor rate had multiplied sevenfold to 42d. in the pound. Aside from a slight dip during the 1770s, the tax burden on the Walthamstow ratepayers grew steadily heavier as the century progressed, averaging 7d. in the pound during the 1720s, 8d. during the 1730s, 11d. during the 1740s, 17d. during the 1750s, 20d. during the 1760s, 18d. during the 1770s, 28d. during the 1780s, and 35d. during the 1790s.

To try to stem this tide of rising poor rates, parish officers during the 18th century both experimented with different management schemes for the workhouse and debated the relative economies of indoor and outdoor relief. At first the Vestry had contracted with various tradesmen to supply the workhouse with food and drink and had hired a governor and governess at an annual salary—Thomas King and his wife in 1726, James Chipperfield and his wife at £10 a year in 1730, John Johnson and his wife Elizabeth at £20 a year in 1742 (Johnson also to act as beadle and his wife to teach the workhouse children to read and write).[24] In September 1753, however, the Vestry moved to control the workhouse costs by agreeing with Richard Haynes, the current master of the workhouse, to feed and clothe the workhouse inmates at a fixed charge per head.[25]

This arrangement had apparently worked well enough for the Vestry to sign a formal contract with Haynes on 25 March 1755:

> Between the Church Wardens And Overseers of the Poor of the parish of Walthamstow
> On the One Part and Richard Haynes On the Other For the space of One Year. Item—
> The said Richard Haynes at his Own Proper Charge to Provide them with Meat Drink
> and Cloaths and all Other Necesarys For their keeping and Maintainance, he the said

Richard Haynes shall be allowd Two shillings And sixpence per week For Each Person. The said Richard Haynes shall be Oblidgd after this agreement Within One Month to Cloath all that is Within the Work house; in Case any Poor Comes into the Work house after this agreement if they want Cloathing to be Cloathd in One Months Time; In Case they stay six months to be Intitled to their Cloaths.[26]

Such contracts, known as 'farming the poor', became commonplace during the second half of the 18th century, as a new breed of entrepreneurs offered their services to parishes throughout the country, bidding against one another for the privilege of running the workhouse at the lowest price per head. In May 1756, in fact, Haynes was underbid by Mr. Tarlan, who offered not only to feed and clothe the inmates, but also to provide bedding, coals, wood, and candles and to keep the brewing vessels and casks in repair—all for the sum of two shillings per head per week.[27]

Not even this system, however, worked for long, as a succession of workhouse masters battled with inflation to honour their contracts, periodically pleading with the Vestry to increase the per capita allowance. In June 1757, for example, Mr. Tarlan was allowed an additional payment of £38 7s. 1d. for cost overruns during the previous year 'in Consideration of the Remarkable Dearness and Scarcety of Bread and Provisions of all kinds' and the price per head was raised temporarily to three shillings per week.[28] In July 1762, Thomas Flack contracted for 2s. 4d. per week, but in December 1764 he was allowed 'two pence per head More for the poor On Acct of the dearness of Allsorts of provisions', and in December 1766 the price per head was again raised to 3s.[29] In March 1769 Flack agreed to lower his price to 2s. 9d., but in February 1771 it returned to 3s., 'Mr Flack Complaining that the High Price of Provisions renders it Impossible for him to Maintain the poor at the present rate of 2s. 9d. per week'. In March 1773 the Vestry ordered 'That a Sum of Five Guineas be given to Mr Flack to help the Cloathing of the poor in the Work house he Complaning that the Dearness of the Several Articles of their Maintainance makes his Contract so hard he cannot go on with it.'[30] In March 1776 Joseph Davis, offering to feed, instruct, and clothe the poor for 2s. 6d. per head, replaced Thomas Flack, but in March 1777 his allowance too had risen to 3s. per head.[31]

Finally, on 20 April 1778, the Vestry established a standing committe to inquire into the state of the poor. Under the leadership of Joel Johnson—London architect, Warden of the Carpenters' Company, and Walthamstow churchwarden between 1778 and 1783—the committee devised new rules for the management of the workhouse, advising the Vestry in March 1780 to return to the former system of direct control of the workhouse by parish officers, hiring a governor and governess, contracting with tradesman for food and supplies, and closely supervising all aspects of the workhouse. In the opinion of the committee,

the Maintanance of the Poor in the Workhouse in a clean Creditable manner with all good & necessary Changes of Uniform food sufficient Cloathing & good sufficient wholesome Diet (as they ought to be now Cloathed & kept by the Present farmer of the

Poor) Together with the Salary & Maintanance of a Sober discreet Master & Mistress of the workhouse whose whole Study & Business should be the Care of the Morals & bodily necessities of the Poor with humanity to them & Oeconomy to the Parish with every Charge included in the head money Per Week now Paid to the farmer of the Poor may be very well done under the Inspection of the Parish Officers (as the same formerly was) at an Expence not Exceeding two Shillings Per head Per Week on an Average.[32]

Accordingly, in July 1780 the Vestry established a new Workhouse Management Committee with sub-committees for 'repairs and furniture of the House, Admission & Discharge of Paupers', for 'the Care of the Morals of the Poor as appointing the Prayers & Lessons to be read Providing Books & seeing that the Children are Properly taught', for 'the Manufactures & setting the Poor to work', for 'Providing Provisions', and for 'Providing Cloathing'.[33] The argument over how to manage the workhouse most economically had come full circle back to where it had begun with the first Walthamstow workhouse in 1726.

    In addition to experimenting with different management schemes, parish officers also debated whether the poor were more economically cared for in or out of the workhouse. Parish policy see-sawed throughout the century, restricting indoor relief when workhouse costs increased and restricting outdoor relief when the cost of pensions increased. Although the annual payments to settled pensioners had dropped dramatically following the establishment of the workhouse and although the payment of this outdoor relief had continued to decline during the 1730s and 1740s, the hope that the workhouse would lead to overall lower poor rates was largely illusory. As outdoor relief decreased, the cost of indoor relief to the poor in the workhouse rose without relief to the ratepayers of Walthamstow. In 1726, during its first year of operation, the workhouse had cost only £57 13s., but costs had doubled during the second year and averaged £111 7s. during the rest of the decade. Between 1736 and 1745 average annual costs increased again by 50 per cent to £167 15s.

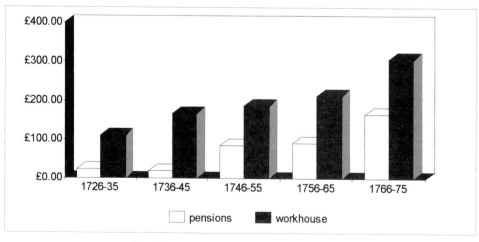

21   Average annual poor relief, 1725-1775.

In January 1747, in an attempt to control the rising costs of the workhouse, the Vestry ordered 'that no person be taken into the said workhouse without an order in writing from a Justice of the peace or Parish Officer'.[34] This order checked the rapid rise in workhouse costs, although the annual average cost continued upwards at a slower pace, rising to £186 12s. between 1746 and 1755 and £212 2s. between 1756 and 1765. Following the law of unintended consequences, however, this Vestry decision had a disastrous effect on the cost of outdoor relief. The number of settled pensioners receiving outdoor relief had averaged only six at any one time during the two decades after the workhouse had opened. After the change in policy in 1747, the number of pensioners doubled in 1748 and by 1753 had doubled again. Average annual costs of outdoor relief rose sharply from a low of £20 between 1736 and 1745 to £85 12s. between 1746 and 1755 and to £92 between 1756 and 1765.

When the cost of pensions again rose sharply to an annual average of £164 2s. during the late 1760s, the Vestry reversed their policy, resolving unanimously on 24 April 1769 'that from and after the 6 Day of May Next That all persons Intitled to Relief from this Parish if they think proper shall Come into the poor house And that no Relief be granted to Any of such poor Persons but from the Apothecary.'[35] This policy reversal, reaffirmed at a Vestry meeting on 15 January 1776, stopped the payment of new pensions, but produced a 45 per cent rise in workhouse costs, which climbed to an annual average of £307 8s. between 1766 and 1775. By April 1779 the policy had changed again with 32 pensioners being paid a weekly total of £5 5s. for outdoor relief, rising to 36 pensioners in October 1779.[36] Either way, whether by outdoor relief to pensioners or by indoor relief to inmates of the workhouse, the poor of the parish had to be housed and clothed and fed. Whichever way the Vestry chose, the cost was going only one way, and that was up.

The dilemma facing the Walthamstow parish officers was shared by church-wardens and overseers of the poor in parishes up and down the country. Nationally, the cost of administering poor law relief has been estimated at between £600,000 and £700,000 in 1700 rising to £4.2 million in 1803—approximately the same sevenfold increase seen in the Walthamstow poor rates.[37] In the end, the dilemma was addressed by a new Act of Parliament in 1782. Entitled 'An Act for the better Relief and employment of the Poor', the statute sought to relieve the tax burden on parish ratepayers by permitting parishes within a ten-mile radius of a central workhouse to unite into a poor law union, by forbidding indoor relief to able-bodied men, and by restricting the workhouse to the impotent poor—the aged, sick and infirm, orphaned children, or children accompanying their mother.[38] Although the workhouse and the fond dream of profitably employing the poor persisted well into the next century, the 1782 statute, by abolishing the 'offer of the house', tacitly acknowledged the failure of the workhouse solution to the problem of caring for the poor.

Five

Life in the Workhouse

GEORGE CRABBE'S POEM *THE VILLAGE*, published in 1783 just one year after Parliament published 'An Act for the better Relief and employment of the Poor', paints a bleak picture of life in the workhouse.[1] Beginning with a realistic, unromanticised description of the hard life of the labouring peasantry, Crabbe continues with the demise of the poor in the parish workhouse, when they have finally grown too old or too sick to work:

> Thus groan the old, till by disease opprest,
> They taste a final woe, and then they rest.
> Theirs is yon house that holds the parish poor,
> Whose walls of mud scarce bear the broken door;
> There, where the putrid vapors flagging, play,
> And the dull wheel hums doleful through the day;
> There children dwell who know no parents' care,
> Parents, who know no children's love, dwell there;
> Heart-broken matrons on their joyless bed,
> Forsaken wives and mothers never wed;
> Dejected widows with unheeded tears,
> And crippled age with more than childhood-fears;
> The lame, the blind, and, far the happiest they!
> The moping idiot and the madman gay.
>
> Here too the sick their final doom receive,
> Here brought, amid the scenes of grief, to grieve;
> Where the loud groans from some sad chamber flow,
> Mixed with the clamours of the crowd below;
> Here sorrowing, they each kindred sorrow scan,
> And the cold charities of man to man.
> Whose laws indeed for ruined age provide,
> And strong compulsion plucks the scrap from pride;
> But still that scrap is bought with many a sigh,
> And pride embitters what it can't deny.

The extent to which Crabbe's poem exaggerates for effect and the extent to which it accurately depicts life in the 18th-century workhouse in general and the Walthamstow workhouse in particular may be gauged through comparison with the hundreds of details in the surviving Vestry minute books, accounts, and other workhouse records that offer glimpses into life inside the Walthamstow workhouse. To be sure many scenes of human misery were played out on the workhouse stage. The Vestry minute on 6 July 1740—'it was ordered as John Danday being absent his four Children should be received into ye Workhouse & to be provided for till further orders'—could well have inspired Crabbe's line, 'There children dwell who know no parents' care'.[2] Either the Vestry minute for 3 January 1742—'Mary Stifte, was orderd to be taken into the Worck House, her Husband Tho: Stifte being run away from her ye 22d December Last passed'—or the entry in Peter Flower's churchwarden's account for

22   Walthamstow Workhouse, erected in 1730.

23   Entrance to the Walthamstow Workhouse.

the same year—'To Ann Wright Late Servant to Dr Adams & gain'd a Settlement in this Parish by said Servitude of 1 year & 3/4 being gott with Child by Wm Dennison promising her marriage, & now he being run away she being in great want of substinance gave her 0.1s.6d.—' could have inspired the lines, 'Heart-broken matrons on their joyless bed, / Forsaken wives and mothers never wed.'[3] Such scenes of human misery were endemic in Walthamstow and in every other parish throughout the country. Nevertheless, for all 'the cold charities of man to man' dispensed by the Walthamstow Vestry, the Walthamstow workhouse did provide the basic needs of life in an age when homelessness, hunger, disease, and unemployment threatened the very existence of the poor.

The workhouse itself, constructed in 1730, was a square eight-room house with a vestry room, two kitchens, pantry and storerooms on the ground floor and bedrooms on the first floor. Outbuildings included a laundry and a brewhouse. An inventory of the workhouse in March 1747 reveals 'foure bedds & bedsteads with two blanketts & a rugg to Each bed & one small Chest' in each of the bedrooms.[4] After the 1756 enlargement of the workhouse, another inventory dated 25 March 1776 reveals 'in the Long Lodging Room' above the workroom '11 Bedsteads 11 Beds 11 Bolsters 11 Coverlids 10 pair of Sheets and 17 Blankets'.[5] The committee formed to inspect the state of the poor reported on 27 November 1779, 'The Officers & Gentlemen present report Viz That having gone over the workhouse & Examined the Rooms & Beds therein did find Beds in the House Sufficient for fifty Persons of the different sexes & Ages as they usually are in proportion' and added 'That there was then in House thirty seven Persons.'[6]

Over the years the workhouse population did not vary greatly. An 'Account of Persons Names & Age in the Workhouse' dated 25 March 1747 lists 34 people, including 2 men aged 60 and 80, 10 women between the ages of 20 and 80, 11 boys between the ages of 5 months and 18 years, and 11 girls between the ages of 1 and 13.[7] Quarterly records entered in the Vestry book for the next seven years show similar results: the total number of residents averaged 30, including several elderly men and women, and the number of infants and children averaged 63 per cent of this figure.[8]

With the workhouse committee in charge, the numbers of inmates did increase, but the nature of the workhouse population remained largely static: a preponderance of deserted or orphaned children, a scattering of unwed mothers or deserted wives with young children, and a handful of elderly men and women. A survey of workhouse inmates by Stracey Till, overseer of the poor, on 10 April 1779 found 44 people in the workhouse, including 6 men aged between 41 and 85, 13 women aged between 21 and 78, 15 boys aged between 6 months and 15 years, and 10 girls aged between 2 months and 15 years.[9]

Among these workhouse residents Crabbe's 'moping idiot' and 'madman gay' are notable by their absence. In fact, the Walthamstow Vestry seems to have sought proper medical care for parish lunatics and the mentally ill. In 1709, for example, the Overseer of the Poor made three journeys to London and spent a total of £2 13s. 6d. in 'getting J Shelly into Bedlam', and in 1723 the Vestry 'Ordered that Mr Jones the Overseer of

the Poore use his endeavour to gett Margarett Stephenson a distracted Pouper placed
in Bedlam at the Parish charge.'[10] The more ordinary medical needs of the Walthamstow
workhouse inmates were cared for by the parish apothecary retained by the Vestry to
'carefully and duely attend, and supply with all proper medicines, The Poor of the said
Parish, not only those in the Workhouse of said Parish, But all Accidental, or other
Poor, as shall be directed by the Church Wardens & Overseers of the said Parish, to
receive Such assistance, and Medicines as aforesaid'.[11] In June 1739 apothecary Robert
Clifton was hired at a salary of 16 guineas, followed by Robert Briscoe in 1747, James
Thornton at a salary of £20 in 1755, and Robert Briscoe again in October 1758 at a
salary of 25 guineas.[12] In November 1777 the Vestry orderd 'that Mr Briscoe the
Apothecary do Regularly attend the poor in the Workhouse Monday and Thursdays
and Admit proper Medicines to those that Are in want and also to Attend at any
Other time When particular Care Requires.'[13] In March 1804, due to 'the Very great
distance of this Parish and the Numerous Poor within it & they are in want of medical
assistance when ill & the great distance for Applying for the same', the Vestry appointed
two 'Medical Gentlemen'—Charles Briscoe and William Price—at salaries of 25 guineas
each, 'to Attend the Poor within the said Parish and to be as Equally divided between
them as near as can be by the Committee to Assist the Parish Officers'.[14] In April 1811
it was further agreed 'that Mr Briscoe should attend the Workhouse and the poor in
the Almshouses and that Mr Price should attend the Rest of the Poor in the Parish'.[15]

New rules established for the workhouse on 26 June 1780 required the surgeon
or apothecary to examine every pauper admitted into the workhouse 'to see that they
are not afflicted with any Infectious Disease & whenever such disorder shall be suspected
they are to be kept alone till he shall report their health & fitness for society.' For his
part the governor of the workhouse was ordered to appoint a room 'for Sick & Lame
men or Boys & another for Sick or Lame Women & Girls' and 'to cause the sick to

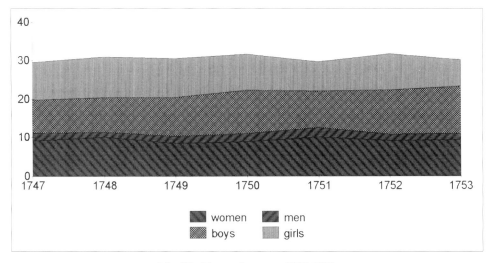

24   Workhouse inmates, 1747-1753.

follow the directions of the Parish Surgeon & Apothecary to whom he is on any disorder appearing on any of the Poor under his care immediately to apply & also if necessary to acquaint the Officers thereof, that in Case of necessity they may be recommended to Proper hospitals.'[16] In January 1814 the Vestry further ordered 'that the churchwardens be requested to procure some plans & estimates for adding to the workhouse a separate apartment for the reception of any paupers afflicted with any Contagious disorders,' and in May 1814 a tender of £229 15s. 2d. for the enlargement was approved.[17] On 15 May 1828 the Vestry considered plans for establishing a dispensary to provide medicines for the poor of the parish.[18] Unlike the hopeless plight of Crabbe's workhouse inmates—'Here too the sick their final doom receive, / Here brought, amid the scenes of grief, to grieve'—the poor of Walthamstow two centuries before the creation of the National Health Service received free medical care under the supervision of the churchwardens and overseers of the poor.

In addition to supplying medical care, the churchwardens and overseers gave the same careful attention to feeding and clothing the poor in the workhouse. At first, the Vestry had contracted directly with butchers, brewers, and bakers to supply the workhouse. During the 1750s and 1760s, when the management of the workhouse was farmed out, the governor of the workhouse had been responsible for feeding and clothing all inmates within his allowed price per head. The menu submitted by Mr. Tarlan in his successful bid to farm the poor for two shillings per head per week relies heavily on porridge, broth, and bread; however, when the Vestry resumed direct control of the workhouse in the late 1770s, the menu improved.[19] In their report on 26 June 1780, the Workhouse Management Committee recommended:

> That the Diet of the Poor shall be as follows: Bread made of second Flour, Beer brewed not to exceed but as near as may be 200 Gallons from 8 Bushells of Malt, Allowance to each Per Day of Beer not to Exceed three Pints in Winter & 4 in Summer, of Meat not less that 8 Ounces for each grown Person on an Average & Children in Proportion, & of other things no Person to be Stinted but a sufficient quantity, but no Waste to be suffered.

To these general recommendations the committee added a menu for the week that would surely have satisfied even a hungry Oliver Twist:

Sunday	Breakfast	Bread & Cheese or Butter
	Dinner	Puddings & Vegetables
	Supper	Bread & Cheese
Monday	Breakfast	Milk pottage or Broth
	Dinner	Puddings or Dumplings
	Supper	Bread & Cheese or Butter
Tuesday	Breakfast	Milk Pottage
	Dinner	Meat & Vegetables
	Supper	Bread & Cheese or Butter

Wednesday	Breakfast	Milk Pottage or Broth
	Dinner	Soup or Milk thicken'd with flour
	Supper	Bread & Cheese or Butter
Thursday	Breakfast	Milk Pottage
	Dinner	Meat & Vegetables
	Supper	Bread & Cheese & Butter
Friday	Breakfast	Milk Pottage or Broth
	Dinner	Pease Soup
	Supper	Bread & Cheese or Butter
Saturday	Breakfast	Milk Pottage
	Dinner	Potatoes & Cold meat or soup
	Supper	Bread & Cheese or Butter

To the menu was appended the option that for suppers all children and anyone else who so wished could substitute milk pottage instead of bread and cheese and butter.[20]

In April 1776 the Vestry also ordered the churchwardens and overseers to provide new clothing for all inmates of the workhouse. Men and boys were each to have a coat, waistcoat and breeches all of the same colour, two shirts, two pairs of stockings, one pair of shoes, and one hat or cap. Women and girls were each to be supplied with one gown, two petticoats, one leather bodice, two pairs of stockings, one pair of shoes, two shifts, two handkerchiefs, two caps, one hat, and two aprons.[21] Under the new rules established in June 1780 the clothing allowance for workhouse inmates also improved:

> The uniform of the Men & Boys to be for each Person Vizt 2 Coats, 2 Waistcoats one of each to be kept clean for Sunday, & the other Coat & Waiscoat for common use all to be made of good Yorkshire Plain of a drab Colour with flat Metal Buttons, & 2 Pair of Russia drab Breeches, three shirts, 3 Stocks, three Pair of Stockens, three Coloured Handkerchiefs, two night Caps, two Pair of shoes, One hat, the Antient Men may have great Coats & the Old women Cloaks if Needfull.

For the women the uniform included

> A Gown & Quilted Petticoat of Linsee the same Colour of the Mens Cloaths, and Extra Gown of the same for Sundays, A Baise Petticoat, A Pair of Leather Bodice, Three shifts, 3 Night Caps, three day caps, 3 Pairs of Stockens, 3 Coloured & 1 white apron, 3 Coloured & 1 white Handkerchief, 2 Pair of shoes, 2 Pockets, a Straw hat.[22]

This workhouse uniform, issued to new inmates on their reception into the work-house, remained the property of the workhouse and had to be returned on their departure. The clothes that each pauper brought into the workhouse were ordered to 'be Aired & Clean'd & if Proper ticketed & laid by for their Use when discharged the House, & also all that are infected with Vermin or supposed to be so are to be Put in

25 Workhouse Account Book: payments to the shoemaker, 1732.

a Sack laid on an Iron frame & baked in an Oven moderately heated till the Vermin are destroyed or Infection removed before they are so laid by'.[23] To identify both the workhouse uniform and the paupers receiving parish relief, the uniform was marked with a P for 'Pauper' and a WP for 'Parish of Walthamstow', a practice first begun in 1741, when at a Vestry meeting on 5 September it was ordered 'That every Person receiving (of this parish) Relief and thir Wives & Children shall vpon the right sleeve of their vppermost Garment wear the Bage of a Roma P & yat said Bage WP be provided by ye Church Wardens & overseers of ye Poor'.[24]

Beyond the immediate physical needs of the workhouse inmates, the church-wardens and overseers of the poor also addressed the inmates' intellectual and spiritual needs. Numerous Vestry orders testify to their concern for the education of the work-house children. The task of teaching often fell to the governess of the workhouse as in 1742, when the governess Elizabeth Johnson was charged with teaching the children reading, writing, and needlework.[25] On 29 August 1776 the Vestry ordered that the current schoolmistress Sarah Snaxton 'For teaching the poor children in the work-house of the Parish be paid One shilling weekly by the Master of the workhouse'.[26]

Following their appointment as governor and governess in 1785, William and Elizabeth Dallet received an annual gratuity of five guineas for teaching the workhouse children to read.[27]

Workhouse rules established in November 1777 had ordered 'That the Children be Taught to read And write and cast Accounts One hour every Morning And the Same every afternoon and Catechisd every Other day And say the Lords prayer And belief every Morning And Night'.[28] After the Workhouse Management Committee was established by the Vestry in June 1780, a much stricter regimen was prescribed both for children and adults. During the summer from Lady Day to Michaelmas rising time was set at half past five and during the winter from Michaelmas to Lady Day at seven o'clock. At six o'clock in the summer and half past seven in the winter the inmates assembled 'clean washed & Dressed' for prayers and reading of the psalm, epistle, and gospel for the day, 'after which every Person shall immediately go to their proper Employment' until breakfast at eight o'clock during the summer and nine during the winter. Half an hour was allowed for breakfast 'after which they shall

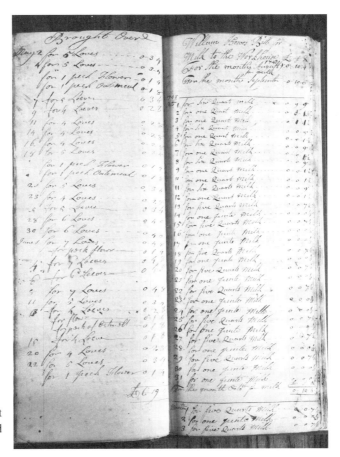

26 Workhouse Account Book: payments for bread and milk, 1743.

diligently apply to work' until noon. An hour was allowed for dinner followed by work again until six o'clock in the summer and five in the winter. Evening prayers and another chapter of scripture were then read, and time was allowed for recreation. Friends could visit or the inmates could 'otherwise carefully employ themselves' until supper at eight o'clock in the summer and seven in the winter followed by bed an hour later. During the winter 'after three in the Afternoon all the Children Boys & Girls shall be instructed in reading & in the first Principles of the Christian religion.'[29] On Sundays the governor and governess were to walk with the workhouse inmates to the parish church, ensuring that

> every Person in health & able Men, women, & Children above four year old (except such only as are necessary to attend the sick) do constantly attend divine service in the Church on every Sunday morning & afternoon & on all holydays, clean washed & dressed & decently seated a Quarter of an hour before Prayers are to begin & stay in their seats till the Congregation is departed.[30]

Following the report to the Vestry on 27 June 1780 by the committee appointed in April 1878 to inquire into the state of the poor, the Vestry approved the comprehensive Rules and Orders for the management of the workhouse and the parish provision for the moral, medical, and physical welfare of the poor. On the same day the Vestry appointed a permanent Workhouse Management Committee 'to assist the Officers and Visit the house to See that the Rules and Orders were Adhered too',[31] thus ensuring that any resemblance between the Walthamstow workhouse and George Crabbe's workhouse would be in name only. On 4 September 1780 a vote of thanks was given to Joel Johnson, churchwarden, 'for the great care & Pains he has taken in conducting the affairs of this Parish', and the Rules and Orders for the workhouse were ordered to be published at parish expense.[32] Reprinted by order of the Vestry 25 years later in January 1807, Joel Johnson's Rules and Orders for the management of the poor continued to ensure the good administration of the workhouse throughout the remainder of the 18th century and well into the 19th century until they were eventually revised in June 1830.[33]

Six

The 18th-Century Charities

THE VESTRY COMMITTEE appointed in April 1778 to inquire into the state of the poor not only examined the management of the parish workhouse, but also turned its attention to the management of the parish charities. Indeed, throughout the 18th century the Vestry, spurred by the constant pressure of rising poor rates, periodically reviewed the terms of the charitable legacies left by Walthamstow's benefactors. In November 1725, for example, the Vestry ordered that

> ye Churchwardens for ye time being shal receive and Collect all rents or profitts as they become due from any Gifts or Charity mony left for ye use of said parish, & yat hee shall apply ye same to such uses as ordered & directed by ye Donors, and yat such Churchwardens from time to time shall make inquiry after all sumes of money yat are or may bee left for ye use of said parrish, and yat have not bene Laid out in lands or applyed in any other manner for ye Benefit thereof, rendering an account thereof from time to time how ye same has bene applyed produceing vouchers for ye same.[1]

In May 1728 a record of 'all ye Gifts yat have bene left to this parish' and 'likewise how ye same have bene directed to be disposed of by ye several Donors' was entered into the Vestry minute book, and it was again ordered that 'ye Churchwardens from this time forward, shall Collect all said Rents, & dispose of yem according to ye wills of ye Donors, keeping a regular Acct thereof yearly with ye parish.'[2] In December 1741 the churchwardens were once again instructed to search diligently for any sums of money left to the parish that had not been accounted for, and churchwarden Peter Flower was ordered to

> Examine at Doctors Commons and other places that he shall think fitt the Coppy of the Will of Sir George Monoux & others whereby it may be seen if the Benefactions & ordinances of Sir George Monoux or of any other Person or Persons who have or shall give Legaceys for the Benefit of said Parish, have been, & Are Properly apply'd according to ye Donor's Will.

During the early 18th-century evidences of the parish charities had been copied into the back of the parish Register of Baptisms, Marriages, and Burials, but in December 1741 the Vestry further ordered 'that a Book be bought & all Wills as aforesaid (& Nothing Else) be Coppy'd in the same'.[3] This book, apparently now lost, probably served as the source of the copy made in 1789 entitled 'Some Particulars relating to the Parish of Walthamstow in the County of Essex Extracted from Authentic Records in the Possession of a late Churchwarden'.[4]

This repeated review of parish legacies by successive generations of parish officers during the 18th century may have been motivated in part by recollection of the inquisitions during the 17th century into the maladministration of the Charity of Thomas Colby and the Charity of Sir George Monoux or by the more recent legal battle with Sir William Scawen over the Charity of Sir Henry Maynard. At the beginning of the 18th century the churchwardens were still pursuing the legacy of Sir Henry Maynard in the High Court of Chancery, and not until 29 November 1720 did the court finally release to the vicar and churchwardens the remaining funds for the purchase of Stretman's Farm.[5] Less successful was the pursuit of the legacy of Matthew Humberstone, a wealthy draper of Humberstone in Lincolnshire, residing in the London parish of St Olaves and maintaining connections with Walthamstow, where his widow Mary Humberstone was buried in St Mary's churchyard after her death on 25 January 1727. By his Will dated 4 March 1708, Matthew Humberstone bequeathed 'unto ye Towne and Parish of Walthamstow in Essex the summe of 10 li. for the use of their poore' and a further sum of £500 for the erection of a schoolhouse and six almshouses. After giving detailed instructions for their construction, Humberstone also directed his executors to expend an additional sum of £600 on the purchase of land sufficient to produce an annual income of £24 to be dispersed in annual stipends of £4 to each of the six almspeople living in the almshouses.[6] On 28 November 1709 the churchwardens obtained a copy of the Will (attested by the executor's clerk to be a true copy), and on 12 November 1711 the Vestry ordered 'that the Church Wardens wait vpon the Executors of Mathew Humberstone Esqr and Claim the Building of a School hous and Six Alms houses as Exprest in the Will for the Parish of Walthamstow'.[7] In the end Mary Humberstone did pay the £10 for the use of the poor, but the remaining bequests for the schoolhouse, the almshouses, and the stipends were never executed.

Yet another lost or lapsed charity came later in the century. In his Will dated 6 August 1764 and proved 24 January 1767, Thomas Beck King left the income arising from four freehold tenements in Walthamstow 'to be laid out in Bread, in such proportion as each honest poor Person belonging to, and living in the Parish of Walthamstow, in the County of Essex, may have one Quartern Loaf every first Lord's Day in the month, throughout the whole year for ever'.[8] This bequest, however, was contingent upon his wife Ann, his son Thomas, his son John, and his kinswoman Judith all dying without heirs. Nothing further is known about this bequest; but, as Vestry Clerk William Houghton commented in 1876, 'In all probability the Testator's

27 List of charitable benefactions copied into the Vestry Minute Book.

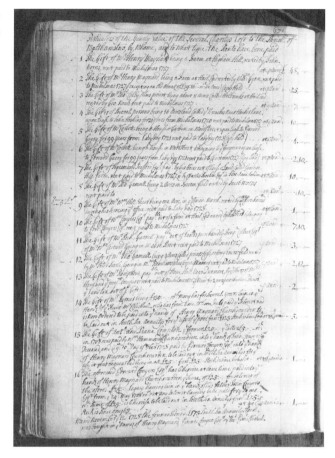

sons, Thomas and John, or his Kinswoman Judith left issue, in either of which cases the Bequest to the Parish would lapse.'[9]

Other 18th-century legacies, however, were successfully added to the parish's growing list of charitable benefactions for the use of the poor. On the west wall of the south aisle in the parish church, the inscription on the Wakelin monument relates that Jeremiah Wakelin, who died on 18 March 1736 aged 74 years, left 'to the poor of this parish for ever about five roods of land called the Pound Field'. In his Will dated 16 June 1735, Jeremiah Wakelin, long-time member of the Walthamstow Vestry and trustee of the Charity of Sir Henry Maynard, left to the churchwardens a field situated near Shernhall Street containing 1 acre, 2 roods and 17 perches, on condition that his family be allowed to possess a pew in the south aisle and to erect a family monument in the church. The £3 annual rent arising from this field was to be distributed to the poor on New Year's Day in bread or meat.[10]

Another legacy for distribution to the poor of Walthamstow came from Thomas Legendre, citizen and Draper of London. In his Will, dated 9 March 1752, Legendre left the following bequest:

Item I Give and bequeath to the Poor that are living in the Parish of Walthamstow Six hundred Pounds of Good and lawfull money of Great Britain to be laid out in a purchase of Lands by the Minister and Church Wardens for the Time being and the Interest or produce thereof to be laid out yearly in Sea Coal for the use and benefit of the Poor that shall live in the Said Parish although not directly the Poor claiming a Right to the Said Parish. I Will and order that within ffourteen days before Christmas Shall be delivered to each poor person no less than two Sacks and not more than three Sacks of Coals forever and it is my desire that Widows be prefered to any others.[11]

This charitable bequest was void by the Statute of Mortmain (9 George II, c.36), but on 8 March 1756 his executor John Fisher gave to the churchwardens £563 12s. Consolidated Bank Annuities to fulfill Legendre's intention.

A third legacy for distribution to the poor, received about the same time, came from Mrs. Catherine Woolball, widow of the late William Woolball, former churchwarden, overseer, and member of the Walthamstow Vestry. In her Will, dated 5 November 1755 and proved on 14 January 1756, Catherine Woolball left 'to the poor of Walthamstow Four Hundred pounds to be put out at Interest in the Names of Trustees to be chosen by the Inhabitants at a Vestry to be Called for that Purpose and the Interest thereof to be Annually applied at Christmas in Every Year for the Benefit of the Poor of the said parish as the Minister And Churchwardens for the Time being shall Direct'.[12] On 23 May 1757 this legacy and the interest accrued was combined with the legacy of Thomas Legendre to purchase a joint sum of £1009 in stock vested in the same trustees, who through the remainder of the 18th century distributed to the poor at Christmas the sum of £30 5s. 4d. according to the wishes of the donors.[13]

Two additional 18th-century charities, left to the churchwardens for the repair of family monuments, were also used at the discretion of the churchwardens for charitable purposes when not needed for their intended purpose. In his Will dated 17 February 1734, Edmund Wise, a merchant of Leyton, left to the churchwardens of Walthamstow lands containing six acres two roods in Low Leyton, today comprising the site of Downsell Road Primary School and residential properties on Toronto Road, Clarence Road, Brierley Road, Langthorne Road and Lynton Road in Leytonstone. In 1734 the land was held on a 41-year lease by Stephen Wood of Low Leyton at an annual rent of £5, and Wise directed that the rent be used by the churchwardens for keeping in repair the Wise family tomb in the south-west corner of Walthamstow parish church.[14] The other bequest came from Thomas Sims, former overseer of the poor, member of the Vestry, and member of the Workhouse Management Committee. In his Will dated 29 July 1782 and proved later that year on 23 December, Thomas Sims left to the churchwardens the sum of £100 to be invested for the repair of his vault and tomb in the Walthamstow churchyard and directed them to 'apply the remainder of such interest to such purposes as they in their discretion should think proper and most beneficial to the said Parish'.[15]

Altogether these five 18th-century charities of Thomas Sims, Edmund Wise, Catherine Woolball, Thomas Legendre and Jeremiah Wakelin yielded an annual income of £41 6s. 6d. during the second half of the century. One further 18th-century bequest, although not a benefaction for the poor, was used in 1715 to erect a table of charitable benefactors in the church. In her Will dated 24 September 1713, Susan Samms had left the residue of her estate 'to be employed in purchasing a Cross branch Candlestick for the use of the Church of Walthamstowe and in Erecting a Turrett upon the Steeple of the said church for hanging therein the Saints bell both these works as well as the care of my Gravestone above mentioned to be committed to the discretion of Mr Edmund Chishull Minister of Walthamstowe'.[16] Endorsed on the Will is a record signed by the Rev. Edmund Chishull concerning the distribution of £44 1s. 10d., being the residue of the estate which passed to the church, which sum was expended on the turret, the candlestick, and a mason's labour for two stone Tables of Benefactions. Upon the receipt of each new charitable benefaction throughout the remainder of the 18th century, the Vestry ordered the name of the benefactor to be inserted in the Table of Benefactions.

This careful monitoring of parish legacies during the 18th century culminated in the work of the Vestry committee appointed on 4 April 1778 to inquire into the state of the poor. Once again the records were searched, the Wills and Trust Deeds of the charitable benefactors examined, and a pamphlet eventually published in 1780 entitled 'An Account of the Benefactions to the Parish of Walthamstow; the Time They Were Given, and Several Appropriations; with the Annual Produce.'[17] During the course of this review Joel Johnson discovered that all the trustees of the Charity of Sir Henry Maynard mentioned in the Trust Deed of 16 August 1734 were dead and that the trust had legally passed to the heirs and survivors of the trustees. Johnson was ordered by the Vestry on 18 October 1779 to 'Proceed in such way as shall appear to him adviseable to procure from the Heir or heirs at Law of the Survivor of the said trustees a Conveyance of said trust Estates.' Accordingly, on 25 March 1780 a new Trust Deed was executed, transferring the ownership of the charity lands from Ellen Flower, Mary Elizabeth Flower and Anne Flower—all heirs of the late Peter Flower, former overseer, churchwarden, and Maynard trustee—to new trustees chosen by the Vestry.[18]

The committee then turned its attention to the Charity of Sir George Monoux. Under the Will of George Monoux, his executors and their heirs were responsible both for the annual payment of £41 14s. 4d. to the almspeople and schoolmaster and for the administration and maintenance of the Monoux almshouses and school. In addition, they were also responsible for the repair of the north aisle of the parish church and the Monoux Chapel, which Monoux had built in the church, and they enjoyed the collection of pew rents and burial fees in that part of the church. As a result, one-third of the parish church was beyond the effective control of the churchwardens and Vestry. On 2 July 1781, calling attention to the 'different Properties in the Parish Church & the great difficulties & Uneasinesses arising therefrom by some of the Inhabitants Paying for their Seats in the Church & others not', the Vestry resolved

'That the Present Officers & Committee for assisting in Managing the House of Industry be a Committee for treating with the different Proprietors & Considering by what ways & Means the whole of the Church may become Parish Property'.[19]

The churchwardens Joel Johnson and John Haffey opened negotiations with the Rev. Edmund Marshall of Charing, Kent, who was then in possession of the London properties in the parish of All Saints, Staining from which the annual rentcharge of £41 14s. 4d. was paid to the schoolmaster and almspeople. In September 1781 letters of agreement were exchanged, and new trustees were appointed by the Vestry for the Sir George Monoux Almshouses. On 6 January 1782 the original rules of George Monoux for the almspeople were carefully revised, and on 13 January the new rules were unanimously approved and 500 copies were ordered to be printed. Eventually, in a Deed of Release signed and dated 30 September 1782, Marshall agreed to relinquish all rights to the administration of the almshouses and school and all rights to property, pew rents and burial fees in the parish church. In turn, the churchwardens agreed to reduce the annual rentcharge of £41 14s. 4d. on the London properties to £21, to make up the remaining sum of £20 14s. 4d. from pew rents and burial fees, and to pay all stipends and administer the almshouses and school according to the original terms of the Monoux bequest.[20]

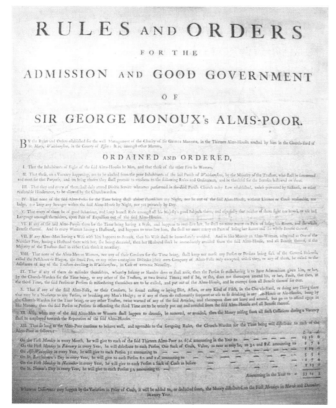

28   Rules for the Sir George Monoux Almshouses, January 1782.

Fifty years later the Commissioners for Inquiring Concerning Charities would criticise the Walthamstow Vestry for this action, remarking,

> It appears indeed to us, that the whole transaction effected by the deed of 1782 was without any sufficient authority and could not be upheld in a court of equity. The parish could have no right to release or convey away any part of the endowment which Sir George Monox had provided for his charity; and though a considerable advantage might be gained to the charity by its being placed under the management of a set of respectable resident trustees, yet this can hardly be considered as an equivalent for the resignation of so large a portion of its funds.[21]

Nevertheless, in 1782 the Vestry had achieved its longstanding ambition of gaining control of the Sir George Monoux Almshouses. Major repairs to the almshouses under the supervision of surveyor Mr. Gibson were begun in September 1787, the expense of £275 0s. 8d. being met by £200 0s. 6d. raised by a voluntary public subscription and the remainder being charged to the poor rates.[22] When Parliament initiated a survey of all charitable donations in England and Wales in 1786, the Vestry and churchwardens for the parish of Walthamstow could point with pride to their administration of 16 charities for the care of the poor producing a clear annual income of £258 0s. 6d.

By far the largest and most significant 18th-century benefaction for the care of the poor, however, was to come in the last decade of the century: the Almshouses and Charity of Mrs. Mary Squire. During 1795 Mrs. Mary Squire, a widow then residing in the parish of St Mary, Newington in Surrey, erected and endowed six almshouses in the parish of Walthamstow 'for the reception from time to time for ever of six poor widows'. Located on the western edge of the churchyard and bordering on the south the workhouse garden and the present day Church Path, the almshouses were built on a piece of land 33 yards in length and 13 yards in breadth, part of a field belonging to John Conyers of Copped Hall. By Indentures of Lease and Release dated 30 and 31 October 1795, John Conyers with the consent of his tenant James Bennett conveyed the piece of land and the six almshouses to the Rev. Edward Conyers of Epping vicarage; John Harman, then lord of the manor of Higham Bensted; and John Rigg, member of the Walthamstow Vestry, overseer in 1802, and churchwarden from 1806 to 1808.[23]

Four days later, by a further Deed of Covenant dated 3 November 1795, Mrs. Mary Squire appointed John Conyers, Edward Conyers, John Harman and John Rigg to be trustees of her almshouses and transferred into their joint names upon trust £550 in three per cent Consolidated Bank Annuities and £550 in three per cent Reduced Bank Annuities. From the interest and dividends arising from these capital sums, Mary Squire directed that £3 be designated annually for the repair of the almshouses and that the remainder be divided 'between the six poor widows who for the time being should under the provisions & directions therein contained be the residents or occupiers of the said six almshouses share & share alike'. The trustees were directed

29   Mary Squire's Almshouses with St Mary's Church in the background, and inset the inscription above the Almshouses.

to act as visitors and governors of the almshouses and to 'elect and place in each one of the said six almshouses a poor widow of a tradesman of the said parish of Walthamstow and no other, such widow being of the age of 50 years and upwards, or younger, being affected in their sight, or lame, when elected'. Whenever the widows resident in the almshouses should die, marry, or be expelled, the trustees were directed to elect others in their place; and whenever any of the four trustees themselves should die or become incapable of acting, the remaining trustees were directed to appoint as a new trustee 'one or more fit and proper person or persons of good credit and reputation Inhabitants of the said parish of Walthamstow' and to transfer the property and money into the joint names of the new trustees.[24]

In her Will, dated 3 February 1796 and proved on 21 March 1797, Mrs. Mary Squire bequeathed £200 to the National School of St Mary's, Walthamstow and to the trustees of her almshouses two further sums of £900 in three per cent Reduced Bank

Annuities and £900 in three per cent Consolidated Bank Annuities. Out of the interest and dividends arising from these latter two investments, Mary Squire directed the almshouse trustees to pay each of the six widows in the almshouses an additional £8 stipend annually, making a total of £13 settled on each almswoman. An additional sum of £6 was to be used every year in October to purchase coal, and the trustees were directed 'to distribute such coals as equally as might be among twelve poor House-keepers of the said parish of Walthamstow who should not be inhabitants of any almshouses in the said parish'. Finally, in her Will Mary Squire repeated her desire that the six almswomen 'might be of the communion of the Church of England, and nowise dissenting therefrom' and that they might strictly adhere to the rules that she had established for the almshouses.[25]

The rules devised, printed, and distributed by Mrs. Mary Squire directed that each widow on her appointment as almswoman be provided with 'a beadstead, a stove, and a large water-tub'. To supplement their stipend, the widows might take in 'one nurse-child, but no more' or 'small washing and clear-starching, but on no account any heavy washing, nor are they to hang out any article whatsoever in front of their houses'. The rules further required that the six widows 'shall attend divine service every Sunday at the parish church of Walthamstow, unless prevented by illness or other reasonable excuse'. The widows were not to receive inmates and 'on no account to permit any man to sleep one night in any of their houses'. Finally, the widows were to conduct themselves decorously at all times, and 'in case they should not be sober and cleanly, or should be quarrelsome, or disturb the peace or quiet of each other, the offender should, after two admonitions, for the third offence be expelled from the almshouse and never again admitted, and another be appointed to succeed her'.[26] Enforcing the rules and paying the stipends stipulated by the Will of Mrs. Mary Squire, the trustees with new additions from time to time over the next century continued to administer the six almshouses according to the wishes of Mrs. Mary Squire until the creation of the Walthamstow Parochial Charities in 1895.

Seven

~~~

Reforming the System

I N 1782 PARLIAMENT had addressed the growing national problem of poor relief in the statute entitled 'An Act for the better Relief and employment of the Poor', also known as Gilbert's Act due to the strenuous efforts of Thomas Gilbert MP to reform the workhouse legislation. This statute permitted parishes within a ten-mile radius of a central workhouse to unite into a poor law union and to appoint visitors and guardians to oversee the workhouse and give orders to the governor regarding diet, clothing, and workhouse routine. Although some parishes took advantage of this cost-cutting measure, the chief impact of the Gilbert Act came from new regulations applying to all parish workhouses. Reversing the 'workhouse test' of the 1723 statute that had forbidden poor relief to any person refusing to enter the workhouse, the 1782 statute forbade indoor relief to all able-bodied men:

> no Person shall be sent to such Poor House or Houses, except such as are become indigent by old Age, Sickness, or Infirmities, and are unable to acquire a Maintenance by their Labour; and except such Orphan Children as shall be sent thither by Order of the Guardian or Guardians of the Poor, with the Approbation of the Visitor; and except such Children as shall necessarily go with their Mothers thither for Sustenance.

The workhouse, then, was restricted to the impotent poor—the aged, sick and infirm, orphaned children, or children accompanying their mother. At the same time the statute directed overseers or guardians of the poor to find work for all unemployed persons able and willing to work and to pay them outdoor poor relief until such time as they could find employment. Finally the statute ordered overseers to prosecute 'all idle or disorderly Persons, who are able, but unwilling, to work or maintain themselves and their Families' and gave justices of the peace power to send such persons to the House of Correction for one to three months.[1]

Although the provisions of the Gilbert Act did control the rapidly rising costs of the parish workhouse, the requirements for paying outdoor relief to unemployed able-bodied men and supplementing low wages simply shifted the tax burden from indoor relief to outdoor relief. As Walthamstow parish officials had discovered earlier in the 18th century, neither restriction of poor relief to workhouse inmates nor increased payment of pensions outside of the workhouse provided an overall solution to the problem of caring for the poor. Rampant inflation during the Napoleonic Wars of the late 18th and early 19th centuries and the Speenhamland ruling by Berkshire magistrates in 1795, indexing outdoor relief to inflation, exacerbated the resulting rise in poor rates throughout the country. Nationally, the expenditure on poor relief by parish officials rose from around £2 million in 1784 to almost £8 million in 1818.[2] In Walthamstow during the fifty years following the Gilbert Act the poor rate doubled from 28d. in the pound in 1782 to 57d. in the pound in 1832. During the same period the total tax raised for poor relief rose fourfold from an annual average of £919 during the 1780s to an annual average of £4,046 during the early 1830s.[3]

Over this period Walthamstow parish officials tried various measures to relieve the ever increasing tax burden on rate payers and to limit the number of paupers claiming poor relief. In June 1815 the Vestry revalued all property in the parish in order to widen the base for assessment of parish rates, establishing ten classes of house ranging from £15 annual rent to £150, three classes of cottage ranging from £3 to £8, three classes of meadow land ranging from £20 to £50, three classes of arable land ranging from £15 to £35, and two classes of marsh land ranging from £10 to £15.[4] Attempting to shame the poor and thus discourage them from claiming relief, the Vestry on 15 March 1819 voted unanimously 'that a list should be printed, within a week after the first Monday in every month containing the Name, Residence, Age, Number of Children, Amount of Relief given, and Cause of such relief being given and that such list should be distributed through the parishes, and also affixed on the Church doors.'[5] In 1820 the parish hired an assistant overseer of the poor to 'take upon himself the whole Management and relief of the Poor, and their Employment

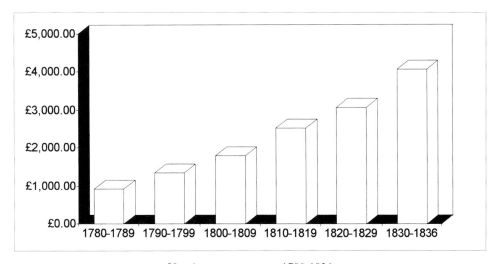

30   Average poor rate 1780-1836.

31   Register of women admitted to the Walthamstow Workhouse in 1828.

in and out of the Workhouse under the superintendance and Control of the Churchwardens & Overseers'. Included among his duties were paying the outdoor poor relief,
visiting the poor in the workhouse and in their own dwellings once every quarter and
advising the churchwardens and overseers on their circumstances, keeping the workhouse accounts, investigating all claims of settlement by paupers, and clearing the
roads of 'Vagrants, Beggars and other improper Characters'. After considering 71
applications, the Vestry hired Thomas Bushel, former master of the Wandsworth
workhouse at a salary of £50 plus board and lodging in the workhouse.[6]

In spite of these various measures and in spite of the statute forbidding indoor
relief to the able-bodied poor, the number of workhouse inmates continued to rise.
When the Vestry undertook another inquiry into the state of the workhouse in October
1828, Thomas Bushel reported 52 persons in the workhouse in 1821, 48 in 1822 and
1823, 53 in 1824, 51 in 1825, 57 in 1826, and 51 in 1827 plus 5 paupers placed out at
houses in the borough and 1 at Stepney Green at a cost of 5s. per week for each plus
an annual clothing allowance of £3. The cost per pauper inside the house averaged five
shillings and sixpence a week.[7] Since the workhouse could conveniently accommodate
only 48 persons, the Workhouse Management Committee recommended on 29 March
1829 the considerable enlargement of the workhouse and a return to the system of
farming the poor, placing the workhouse 'under the Superintendance of a competent
Master & Matron who shall contract for the maintenance of the poor & be entitled
to the benefit of their labor'.[8] In the end, however, relief came from an unexpected
quarter: the Poor Law Amendment Act 1834, the first of two national reforms during
the 1830s that radically changed the provision for the poor in Walthamstow.

In February 1832 a Royal Commission had been established to investigate the poor law problem. The subsequent Poor Law Report published in 1834 advocated that two principles form the foundation of future poor law reform: the principle of 'the workhouse test' and the principle of 'less eligibility'. According to the first principle, all outdoor relief to able-bodied workers and their families would be abolished: 'All relief whatever to able-bodied persons or to their families, otherwise than in well-regulated workhouses ... shall be declared unlawful.'[9] The principle of 'less eligibility' required that the condition of workhouses inmates be less favourable than that of the lowest-paid labourers outside the workhouse:

> making this workhouse an uninviting place of wholesome restraint, preventing any of its inmates from going out or receiving visitors, without a written order to that effect from one of the overseers, disallowing beer and tobacco, and finding them work according to their ability: thus making the parish fund the last resource of a pauper, and rendering the person who administers the relief the hardest taskmaster and the worst paymaster that the idle and the dissolute can apply to.[10]

Generally based on the principles laid down in the Poor Law Report, the Poor Law Amendment Act, which received Royal Assent on 14 August 1834, for the first time established a centralised administrative structure for poor law relief. Three poor law commissioners were appointed, and the country was divided into nine divisions each headed by an assistant commissioner who grouped the parishes in his division into poor law unions. Each union was to elect a board of guardians, who would

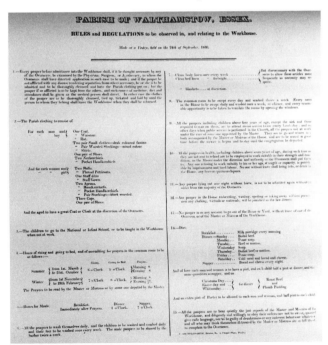

32 Walthamstow Workhouse rules and regulations, September 1830.

employ a clerk to the board and a staff of relieving officers, workhouse masters, assistant overseers, poor rate collectors, and district medical officers. Relief was to be administered in the workhouse, except in cases of physical infirmity, and conditions inside the workhouse were to be less favourable than those for persons outside the workhouse.

In March 1836 an information meeting was held at *The Swan* in Stratford, called by Alfred Power, assistant poor law commissioner for the south-east, to explain the proposed poor law union. Two months later Robert Cotesworth, Walthamstow overseer of the poor, received the order from the Poor Law Commissioners, dated 16 May 1836, establishing the West Ham Union of the parishes of West Ham, Walthamstow, Low Leyton, Woodford St Mary, East Ham, Wanstead and Little Ilford, for the administration of the laws for the relief of the poor.[11] A Board of Guardians was to be elected to meet weekly to make all decisions necessary regarding paupers and to give instructions to the parish officers. The poor law union was to appoint a clerk, treasurer, relieving officers, and medical officers. Churchwardens and overseers of the poor were still to make and collect the poor rates and pay them over to the board of guardians. They were allowed to give temporary relief 'in any case of sudden and urgent necessity', but it had to be reported in writing to the board of guardians, to whom all paupers would subsequently apply for relief. From 23 July 1836 the following rules were to be binding upon the parishes:

> Firstly. No relief shall be given in money (except in cases of sickness or accident) to any able-bodied male pauper, who is in employment (the same not being parish work), and in the receipt of earnings; nor to any part of his family who shall be dependent on him, or for whose relief and maintenance he shall be liable.

> Secondly. If any able-bodied male pauper shall apply to be set to work by the parish, one half at least of the relief which may be afforded to him or to his family shall be in kind.

> Thirdly. One half at least of the relief which may be afforded to widows or single women, not being aged or infirm, shall be in kind.

> Fourthly. No relief shall be given to any able-bodied male pauper by payment or payments, of, for, or on account of the rent for his house or lodging, or for the house or lodging of any part of his family who shall be dependent upon him, and for whose relief and maintenance he shall be liable, or by allowance towards such rent.

> Fifthly. Except in case of accident, sickness, or other urgent necessity, no relief shall be afforded from the poor-rates of any parish or place comprised in the said Union, to any pauper between the ages of sixteen and sixty, belonging to any such parish or place comprised in the said Union, who shall not be resident therein: Provided always that this regulation shall not extend to any person not being an able-bodied male pauper between the ages of sixteen and sixty, who shall, on the day herein appointed for the first meeting of the Guardians, be in the receipt of relief from any parish or place comprised in the said Union, although not resident in such parish or place, and although such person shall continue a non-resident: but in every such case due enquiry shall be made as to the propriety of such relief being continued.

33   The Board of Guardians of the West Ham Poor Law Union.

Further orders came from the Poor Law Commissioners on 5 August 1836 for setting up record-keeping proceedures for the West Ham Poor Law Union beginning on 29 September, including minute books and ledgers for the board of guardians, the pauper description book, the weekly relief book for out-door paupers, the admission book for in-door paupers, rate books, workhouse records, and various report forms.[12] On 2 January 1837 Thomas Barker of Wanstead, the new rate collector for the parishes of Walthamstow, Leyton, Woodford and Wanstead, began to collect the rates and pay them to the treasurer of the union.[13] This time the rate relief was real. With seven parishes supporting one workhouse, poor rates in Walthamstow dropped from 60d. in the pound in 1836 to 24d. in the pound in 1839 and remained at that level for most of the next decade.[14]

The new poor law union continued temporarily to operate the workhouses at Woodford, West Ham and Walthamstow, while the new union workhouse was under construction in Leytonstone. After the removal of inmates to the union workhouse was complete, however, the Walthamstow workhouse was used by the Vestry and parish officers, and in August 1842 part of it was leased to the Metropolitan Police. Eventually transferred by the churchwardens, along with other charity property, to the Walthamstow Charity Governors in 1880, the building was let to the Literary and Scientific Institute in 1882 and then to private tenants. In 1930 Miss C. Demain Saunders transferred the remainder of her lease of Vestry House to the Borough of

Walthamstow for the building to be used as a local history museum, and in 1944 the trustees of the Walthamstow Parochial Charities sold the building to the corporation, ending over two hundred years of charity involvement with the parish workhouse.[15]

Throughout the remainder of the 19th and the beginning of the 20th century, the board of guardians of the West Ham Poor Law Union continued to care for Walthamstow's paupers. Administered nationally by the Poor Law Board from 1847 to 1871, poor law unions, along with responsibility for public health, passed to the Local Government Board in 1871. Although the Local Government Act 1888 created county councils and the Local Government Act 1894 created urban and rural district councils, neither new body assumed control for poor law unions, which continued to function with official duties and geographical boundaries often overlapping those of the new local authorities. Another Royal Commission, appointed in 1905 to examine the administration of the poor laws, recommended the abandonment of both the principle of the workhouse as a deterrent and the principle of less eligibility. By the beginning of the 20th century, comments Pauline Gregg, 'less eligibility and the work-house test had been gradually abandoned in face of growing unemployment, and a slowly dawning realization that harsh workhouse conditions could not make the sick well, the infirm agile, or the workless employed'.[16] No longer seeking to intimidate or shame paupers, government officials in the 20th century began to seek new solutions to prevent and cure poverty. The Old Age Pensions Act 1908 created universal pensions for the elderly, and unemployment insurance legislation was enacted in 1911. Eventually the Local Government Act 1929 abolished the boards of guardians, almost one hundred years after their creation, and gave to county and urban councils responsibility for administering poor relief.

In addition to the reform of the poor laws in 1834, a second national reform also radically changed the provision for the poor in Walthamstow during the 1830s: the Brougham Commission for Inquiring Concerning Charities. During the 1780s Thomas Gilbert MP had initiated not only the reform of workhouse legislation but also the reform of charity legislation. Through his efforts legislation had been passed in 1786 launching an enquiry into charities in England and Wales. The subsequent report submitted to the House of Commons on 10 June 1788 had concluded that 'many of the said Charitable Donations appear to have been lost: and that many others of them, from neglect of payment, and the inattention of those Persons who ought to superintend them, are in danger of being lost, or rendered very difficult to be recovered'; and the report had urged the 'serious and speedy attention of Parliament' to establish 'such measures as may be effectual for the relief of the Poor Persons who were the objects of those Donations, and for carrying the charitable and benevolent purposes of the Donor into execution'.[17] The report lists county by county and parish by parish all charities for relief of the poor, giving the purpose of the charity, the trustees of the charity, and the annual income of each charity from land or money. Eventually published in 1816 under the title 'Abstract of the Returns of Charitable Donations for the Benefit of Poor Persons made by the Ministers and Churchwardens of the Severall

34 Walthamstow Charity Accounts required by the Charity Commissioners, 1853.

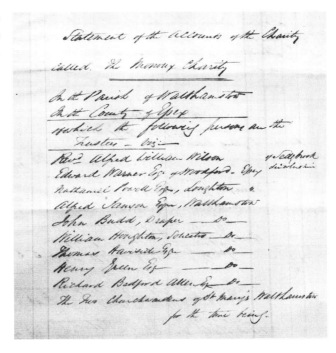

Parishes and Townships in England and Wales', the report reveals a total annual charitable income from nearly 13,000 parishes and townships in England and Wales of £258,710 19s. 3d. Thanks largely to the conscientious efforts of the Vestry and churchwardens to maintain the Walthamstow charities, throughout the 18th century the parish of Walthamstow reported 16 charities with a total annual income of £256 7s. 3½d. in 1786, an amount well above the national average.[18]

Following the publication of this report in 1816, a national commission of inquiry on educational charities was appointed in 1818 through the efforts of Henry, Lord Brougham, Scottish barrister, statesman and philanthropist, followed by another commission in 1819 to investigate all the charities for the poor in England and Wales. Subsequent commissions continued their inquiries year by year until 1835, when a House of Commons Select Committee made a strong report advocating the establishment of a permanent and independent charity board to inquire into the administration of all charities, to compel the production of accounts, and to secure the safe custody of charity property. Another commission followed in 1849, leading eventually to the Charitable Trusts Act 1853, which established The Charity Commissioners of England and Wales.[19]

The Brougham Commissioners for Inquiring Concerning Charities began their investigation of the Walthamstow charities in 1831. The churchwardens and charity trustees were summoned to appear before the Commissioners at Great George Street, Westminster, to give information concerning each parish charity. All charity Deeds, Leases, extracts from Wills, and other evidences collected by the churchwardens over the years were inventoried, numbered, and submitted along with the charity and church accounts to the Commissioners for inspection early in 1832.[20] The resulting Report of the Commissioners for Inquiring Concerning Charities, dated 10 July 1832 and printed on 11 March 1833, presents the fullest and most detailed account up to that time of the Walthamstow charities.[21]

As well as investigating the source and purpose of each charity, the Report of the Commissioners analysed the application of charity income and criticised the Walthamstow churchwardens for certain misapplications of charity funds. The Deed of 1782 reducing the annual rentcharge received for the Charity of George Monoux from £41 14s. 4d. to £21 was judged to be 'without any sufficient authority and could not be upheld in a court of equity'. The deficiency of £20 14s. 4d., which by terms of the 1782 Deed should have been made up by the churchwardens from pew rents and burial fees, had been for the most part 'supplied from other charitable funds in the possession of the parish'. Bluntly stating 'it is clear that the parish had no right to supply such deficiency out of other charitable funds of which they had been made trustees for the benefit of the poor', the Commissioners advised the parish to raise a sum of money sufficient to pay an annual return of £20 14s. 4d. and settle such sum on the trustees of the Monoux Charity. 'If this, or some measure of a similar nature and effect, be not adopted by the parish,' concluded the Commissioners, 'it must be a matter of consideration whether steps ought not to be taken to set aside the Deeds of 1782.'[22] While noting that not all of the income of the Charity of James Holbrook had been annually spent in bread according to the terms of the donor and that improper payments had been made from the income of the Inhabitants' Donation, the Commissioners reserved their sharpest criticisms for the large balances often maintained on the charity accounts and the traditional custom practised by generations of Walthamstow churchwardens of transferring charity income to the general church-wardens' account—a practice that for over a century had been followed to subsidise the payment of poor relief and to reduce the deficit chargable to the poor rates. 'We cannot but animadvert upon the blameable inattention to the due application of these charitable funds, which has permitted such large balances to be diverted year after year from their proper destination to the general purposes of the church account.'[23] Although the parish apparently did not follow the Commissioners' recommendation concerning the Monoux Charity, the forceful charges of misapplication of charitable funds, together with the Poor Law Amendment Act 1834 which relieved the church-wardens and overseers of the poor from dispensing poor relief, did in the end reform the churchwardens' accounting procedures for distributing the income from parish charities. Beginning in 1858, the new Charity Commissioners for England and Wales appointed under the Charitable Trusts Act 1853 required the Walthamstow church-wardens and charity trustees, along with all other charity trustees throughout the country, to submit annual accounts, thus ensuring that all future income from the Walthamstow charities during the remainder of the 19th and 20th centuries would be distributed according to the wishes of Walthamstow's benefactors.[24]

Eight

———❧———

The 19th-Century Charities

WHILE NATIONAL REFORMS altered the administration of poor relief and the accountability of charity trustees, Walthamstow benefactors continued throughout the 19th-century to make new charitable donations for the care of the poor. Following the lead of earlier benefactors, new parish charities were established for the distribution of bread and coal. By a Deed Poll dated 15 March 1782, James Holbrook, a brewer residing in the parish of Saint Botolph without Aldgate, had created a charity for the distribution of bread to the poor of Walthamstow:

> I, James Holbrook, being desirous to assist the poor of the parish of Walthamstow in the County of Essex, do request the minister and Church Wardens for the time being of the said parish during my Life Time to employ such Baker in the said parish as the Major part of them shall agree upon to Bake Weekly Ten Sixpenny Wheaten Loaves, which Loaves I desire the said Minister and Church Wardens to order to be distributed in the parish Church of Walthamstow aforesaid on every Lords Day immediately after the Morning Divine Service is over to Ten poor persons of the said parish who shall be by them deemed most in want.[1]

To make his charity permanent, on 30 September 1805 James Holbrook conveyed to trustees an annual rent-charge on land that he owned on Marsh Street in Walthamstow and directed that £39 be paid yearly to the minister and churchwardens of Walthamstow.[2] A further Deed, signed and dated 25 April 1807, substituted for the sixpenny loaves 'Ten Quartern Loaves of the best Wheaten Bread to Ten Poor Aged People living in or belonging to this parish', and stipulated that after his decease 'the Baker's to be paid half Yearly by James Richardson or some one of his Executors or the next Heir at Law from the Farm at Walthamstow now in the occupation of Mr Robert Woodman.'[3]

Later in the century William Cluff, a wealthy Walthamstow silk manufacturer, established a further charity for the distribution of coal and bread at Christmas. In his Will, made 11 February 1874 and proved 18 June 1874, Cluff left to the vicar, church-wardens, and overseers of the poor the sum of £1,000, directing that 'the dividends

and Income thereof be applied every Christmas in giving to thirty poor deserving
people living in the said Parish of Walthamstow five sacks of good Coals each and
so much bread as the balance of the said dividends and income will purchase after
payment of the said Coals to be equally divided between them'.[4] The report of William
Houghton to the Vestry on 25 August 1876 records expenditure of £31 2s. 3d. for
bread and coals in the previous year from the Gift of William Cluff.[5]

Other 19th-century Walthamstow charities were established to maintain family
monuments in the church or churchyard with the surplus not needed for maintenance
to be expended on the poor generally. John Rigg, for example, whose family for several
generations had served as churchwardens, overseers of the poor, and charity trustees,
in 1806 left to the vicar and churchwardens £20 for the poor of the parish and £100
to be invested to keep his family vault in repair. The annual income of £3 during the
19th century, when not needed for maintenance of the monument, was carried to the
general charity account.[6]

On 20 February 1838 Elizabeth Cass left the large sum of £4,000 to the vicar and
churchwardens to use the annual interest and dividends 'to repair and keep in repair
our family tomb in Walthamstow Church Yard' and to divide the remainder 'amongst
as many poor persons of good character not receiving parochial relief and members
of the Established Protestant Church of England as they the said Vicar and Churchwardens shall think fit'.[7] The inscription on the Cass monument reads in part: 'Within
this vault are deposited the remains of Elizabeth Cass. She was a liberal benefactress
to many charitable institutions but especially to the parochial schools and the poor of
this parish, where she passed the last years of her truly Christian life, and died in hope
of a better world, February 20th 1838.'[8] For their trouble in administering this bequest,
Elizabeth Cass further bequeathed an annual payment of £30 to be divided among the
vicar and churchwardens.

Later that same year, in his Will dated 8 May 1838, John Morley, formerly of
Walthamstow, directed his executors and trustees to erect a monument at the cost of
£300 over the vault in the Walthamstow churchyard containing the remains of his
father and mother. He further directed his executors to establish a fund of £300
invested in three per cent Consolidated Bank Annuities and to use the annual interest
of £9 in 'discharging the expenses of preserving and keeping in good order and repair
of the said vault and monument and also of the tablet in the church to the Memory
of my Mother'. Any surplus not needed for this purpose Morley requested 'be paid
to the Rector and churchwardens for the parish of Walthamstow to be by them
applied on the seventeenth of April in every year (that being the day of my birth) in
the distribution of Bread to such poor persons of the parish as the Rector and Churchwardens may think best qualified to receive the same'.[9] After Morley's death on
21 September 1845, the churchwardens experienced difficulty in collecting this bequest
from Morley's executors and trustees. Eventually, however, on 30 April 1857 a Bill of
Complaint by Morley's niece and heir initiated proceedings in the High Court of
Chancery to settle the estate and provide for payment of the annuity. Three years later

a Court of Chancery Decree dated 14 July 1860 finally ordered the surviving trustees to transfer the £300 Consolidated Bank Annuities into the name of the Accountant General to be held in trust in 'an account to be entitled "The Vault Monument and Tablet Account"' with the dividends to be paid to the vicar and churchwardens for the purposes described in the Will.[10]

Not connected with the maintenance of monuments, other 19th-century charities, both specific and general, were also established for the benefit of the poor. By her Will dated 1 December 1810, Mary Newell bequeathed to her executors the sum of £500 three per cent Consolidated Bank Annuities upon trust to distribute the annual dividends for the apprenticeship and education of poor children in Walthamstow. Two-thirds of the annual dividends were to be paid to the churchwardens 'for the purpose of yearly binding out apprentice one boy belonging to the said parish, who should be the son of parents of the Established Church of England, and should be approved of by the minister for the time being of the said parish'. The remaining one-third of the annual dividends was to be paid to the treasurer 'of the Sunday school of the Established Church at Walthamstow aforesaid, for the purposes of that institution'.

35 Monument erected by John Morley in St Mary's Church.

When the Commissioners for Inquiring Concerning Charities investigated this charity in 1832, they reported that, 'A poor boy, the child of a parishioner, selected by the churchwardens, with the approbation of the vicar, is annually put out apprentice with this benefaction. The premium of £10 is sufficient for most of the trades to which the children are apprenticed.' The Commissioners further noted that, 'The £5 is paid to the treasurer of the National school, for the maintenance of a Sunday school connected with that establishment.'[11]

A more general charity for the poor was established by Daniel Maclaurin. In his Will, dated 21 April 1868 and proved on 9 October 1877, Daniel Maclaurin left the sum of £150 to the rector of the parish of Walthamstow to invest in three per cent

Consolidated Bank Annuities and to distribute the annual dividends among the poor of the parish. In December 1901 the trustees of the Walthamstow Parochial Charities sold most of this stock and purchased for £120 a piece of land on the north side of Havant Road adjoining in the rear land on Wyatt Lane belonging to the Charity of Edward Corbett. The houses erected on this land, known today as No. 40 to No. 52 Havant Road, were sold by the trustees between 1969 and 1980 for over £5,000 and the money re-invested.[12]

The remaining 19th-century charities established by Walthamstow benefactors were devoted to the almshouses of the parish. Several new charities supported the Monoux and Squire almshouses by increasing the stipends paid to the elderly poor residents. On 22 September 1812, for example, Richard Banks, former overseer of the poor in 1799 and long-time Vestry clerk, added a Codicil to his Will directing that his wife during her lifetime should receive the interest and dividends from £800 Navy five per cent Bank Annuities and that after her death the interest and dividends should be paid for ever to the churchwardens and by them divided 'equally to and amongst the Poor of the Alms-houses, in the said Parish of Walthamstow, commonly called, or known by the name of Sir George Monox's Alms-houses'.[13] This bequest, reduced by legacy duty to £720, came into possession of the churchwardens in 1825; and in 1832 the Commissioners reported that the annual dividend was £26 9s. 2d., making an additional annual stipend of £2 0s. 8d. for each almsperson.[14]

The stipends of Monoux almsfolk were also increased through the Charity of John Harman, lord of the manor of Higham Bensted and trustee of the Mary Squire Almshouses. In his will dated 27 October 1815, John Harman left to his son Jeremiah Harman £200 to be distributed at his discretion to the poor residing in or near the parish of Walthamstow. By a Codicil to his Will dated 28 July 1817 this bequest was doubled, and Jeremiah Harman subsequently added an additional £100, making a total of £500, which he divided £100 to the parish of Woodford, £50 to the parish of Chingford, and £350 to the parish of Walthamstow. At Christmas 1817 Jeremiah Harman, after consulting the Walthamstow churchwardens, distributed £65 among the poor of the parish, adding a further gift from himself of £5 to each almswoman in the Mary Squire Almshouses 'as a token of remembrance to them from my Father who had for many years been the acting Trustee of that Charity'. On 26 December 1818 he transferred the remaining £285 to the churchwardens, which they invested in £273 Navy five per cent Bank Annuities producing an annual dividend of £13 13s. 0d. By a unanimous vote of the Vestry on 15 March 1819, the dividend was 'appropriated for the better maintenance of the 13 Alms poor in Sir George Monox Alms houses,' adding another guinea to the annual stipend of each almsperson.[15]

A third bequest for the support of the Monoux almspeople came from Walthamstow resident William Bedford. By a Codicil to his Will dated 6 June 1822, Bedford left to the vicar, Vestry clerk, and 'some one other respectable inhabitant of the same parish to be named by his executors' £500 four per cent Bank Annuities 'for the benefit of the poor belonging to Monox's almshouses at Walthamstow'.[16] From

36 Monument of Robert Barker in St Mary's churchyard.

the £20 annual dividend Bedford directed that 15 shillings should be paid to each of the 13 almsfolk at half-yearly intervals, making a total of £19 10s., and that the remaining 10s. should be used by his trustees for the repair and maintenance of his family vault in the churchyard. In 1832 the Commissioners reported that the income from these three bequests of Bedford, Harman, and Banks, together designated in the accounts as 'the auxiliary bequests to the Monox almspeople', amounted to an annual total of £65, making an additional annual stipend of £5 for each almsperson to supplement the original bequest of George Monoux.

Not only the Monoux almsfolk, but also the almswomen of the Mary Squire's Almshouses benefited from Walthamstow's 19th-century benefactors. In her Will dated 15 April 1834 and proved 29 April 1842, Elizabeth Collard, widow of James Collard, bequeathed to her nephew George Collard, to her nephew Thomas Collard, to the vicar of Walthamstow, and to the trustees of the George Monoux Almshouses and the trustees of the Mary Squire's Almshouses the sum of £500 'Upon trust to pay the interest thereof every half year to the poor persons inhabiting the same Alms Houses share and share alike'.[17] Further help for the Mary Squire's Almshouses came from the auxiliary bequest of Robert Barker. On 29 March 1856 the Rev. William Wilson and Robert Vigne, the two surviving trustees of the Charity of Mrs. Mary Squire, appointed the Rev. Thomas Parry, vicar of Walthamstow, and Robert Barker, Esq. of Walthamstow to be new trustees in place of Edward Forster and Francis Robert Bidwell then deceased.[18] Sometime during his trusteeship Robert Barker added £100 stock to each of the sums of £1,450 three per cent reduced Bank Annuities and £1,450 three per cent Consolidated Bank Annuities originally given by Mrs. Mary Squire to support her almshouses and to pay stipends to her almswomen.[19] A third bequest for the benefit of the Squire's almswomen came from Mrs. Mary Cox, whose Will dated 3 August 1878 was proved on

30 April 1889. In memory of her family, whose monument stands in the Walthamstow churchyard, Mrs. Mary Cox gave to the rector for the time being the sum of £150:

> Upon trust to invest the same in his name in the Three pound per cent Consolidated Bank Annuities and to apply and distribute the annual dividends arising therefrom amongst the six aged women who for the time being are the occupants of the said almshouses in the Churchyard of the said parish of Walthamstow to be divided equally amongst such occupants.[20]

Together with the original endowment by Mrs. Mary Squire, these three additional 19th-century bequests were yielding a total annual income of £94 3s. 4d., when administration of the Mary Squire's Almshouses passed to the trustees of the Walthamstow Parochial Charities in 1895.[21]

By far the largest and most significant almshouse bequest of the 19th century came from Mrs. Jane Sabina Collard, by whose generosity 10 almshouses were erected in 1881 for 'poor and deserving men none of whom shall be aged less than sixty years and none of whom shall have been at any time engaged or employed as a domestic servant or in the receipt of parochial relief'.[22] On 18 May 1859 Mrs. Jane Sabina Collard conveyed to three trustees—Arthur Foulger, Charles Richard Vines and William Houghton—a piece of land on the south side of Shernhall Street known as Pound Field and two pieces of land, each 250 feet by 70 feet, on the north and south sides of Maynard Road. In this Trust Deed Mrs. Collard instructed the trustees to accumulate and invest the proceeds from these properties and within 21 years to use the accumulated funds, together with any other gifts or moneys that the trustees might acquire, for the erection and endowment of almshouses.

By August 1876, when William Houghton reported to the Vestry on the state of the Walthamstow charities, the trustees had invested the accumulated rents in stock worth £338 15s. 4d., purchased an additional piece of land adjacent to the Pound Field, and showed an annual income of £37 0s. 5d. from their property and investments.[23] Jane Sabina Collard had died on 27 October 1862, leaving in her Will extensive personal bequests to the three trustees of her almshouse charity. Following the death of her second husband Thomas Jones Burton, the trustees received these bequests between 1876 and 1881. Since the Will of Mrs. Jane Sabina Collard made no mention of her almshouses, two of the three trustees claimed that the additional bequests were personal gifts rather than gifts in trust for the almshouses. William Houghton, however, believed that the bequests had been made in trust for the almshouses and persuaded Arthur Foulger to give part of his share to the Collard Charity. With the accumulated dividends and rents of the original endowment, supplemented by £3,209 from William Houghton and £1,000 from Arthur Foulger, the Collard almshouses were finally erected in 1881, a single-storey range of 10 brick almshouses with a central gabled porch situated on the north side of Maynard Road and east of Beulah Path. A Trust Deed dated 19 October 1882 officially established the Charity of Jane Sabina Collard with the auxiliary endowments of Arthur Foulger and William Houghton and appointed William

37 Jane Sabina Collard Almshouses, erected in 1881.

Houghton, Gilbert Houghton and William E. Whittingham as new trustees. Over the next decade the trustees invested the remaining funds, purchasing property known as Carlton Terrace on Hoe Street in 1883, property known as Hope Cottages on Cottenham Road in 1885, and six houses known as Halwyn Villas on Albert Road in 1889.[24] By April 1890 the trustees reported annual receipts from interest, dividends and rents of £186 10s. 5d.; total expenses of £180 10s. 1d., including monthly stipends of 16s. to each of the 10 almsmen; and a total capital account balance of £1,836 9s. 6d.

Throughout the 19th century, then, the Walthamstow charities both consolidated and expanded their resources to care for the poor, as new benefactors supplemented existing almshouse charities and established additional almshouses and charities for the distribution of bread and coal. In 1786 the Gilbert survey had revealed a total annual income of £256 7s. 3d. from the Walthamstow charities. In 1876 William Houghton's report to the Walthamstow Vestry revealed a total annual income of £1,166 7s. 11d. By the end of the 19th century, when the Charity Commissioners had consolidated all the Walthamstow parish charities under one administration, the total annual income arising from rents and dividends had increased still further to £1,709 16s.[25] The generous donations and careful stewardship of the Walthamstow charities during the 19th century were reaping rewards. For parish officials and charity trustees in the closing decades of the 19th century, however, the application of this steadily increasing charity income would pose the greatest challenge and the greatest source of contention.

Nine

— · ⊰⊱ · —

Walthamstow Charity Governors

NEITHER THE GENEROSITY OF WALTHAMSTOW BENEFACTORS nor
the increasing charity income devoted to the almshouses and distributed annually
in bread and coals prepared the parish for the dramatic changes resulting from the
rapid increase in the Walthamstow population during the 19th century. From a village
population of 3,006 in 1801 Walthamstow had mushroomed to an urban population
of 96,720 in 1901. Between 1851 and 1871 the population had more than doubled
from 4,959 to 11,092, and during every succeeding decade it doubled again, reaching
22,531 in 1881, 47,154 in 1891, and 96,720 in 1901.

The increasing population of Walthamstow inevitably led to parochial and political
change. The ancient parish of St Mary had been divided in 1844, creating the three
new parishes of St Peter, St James and St John. The population explosion during the
latter quarter of the century brought further parochial expansion with the creation of
the parish of St Saviour out of St James in 1875, the parish of St Stephen partly out
of St Mary in 1881, and the parish of St Michael and All Angels out of St Saviour
in 1887. In 1873 the newly created Walthamstow Local Board assumed the secular
functions of the old Walthamstow Vestry, including the Highway Board, the Nuisance
Removal Committee, and the Sewer Authority; and following the passage of the Local
Government Act 1894, Walthamstow became an Urban District Council. During the
1870s, however, the Vestry still retained the power to collect poor rates; and chiefly
through the vicar, churchwardens, and overseers of the poor it still controlled the
increasingly wealthy and increasingly controversial parochial charities.

Moreover, the Walthamstow population was not only increasing dramatically, it
was also changing character during the latter half of the 19th century. The sharp
division between wealthy landowners living in country houses and poor labourers
working on manorial estates was disappearing. The arrival of the Great Eastern Railway
in the early 1870s meant that more city clerks and white collar workers were settling
in the district. Fears were expressed among this growing middle class, perhaps with
some justification, that the generous annual distribution of bread and coals was
attracting pauperism into Walthamstow and building up a class of improvident people

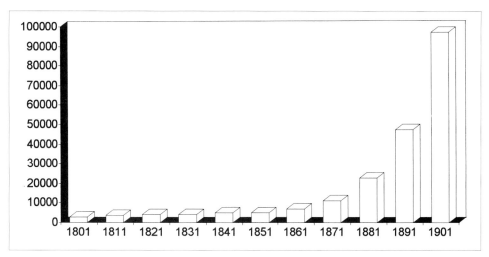

38   The Walthamstow population, 1801-1901.

who inevitably ended up on the poor relief rolls at the expense of the parish, when
accidents happened or employment ceased. The parochial charity accounts for 1877-8,
for example, show general distributions of bread amounting to £197 18s. and coal
amounting to £129 15s. 2d., in addition to the stipends paid directly to the almspeople
in the Monoux and Squire almshouses.[1] In spite of such generous charitable
benefactions, the number of Walthamstow paupers receiving indoor relief in the
workhouse or outdoor relief in the parish had increased considerably since the formation
of the West Ham Poor Law Union in the 1830s. In 1837 an average of 86 Walthamstow
men, women, and children had received indoor relief and 228 had received outdoor
relief.[2] Forty years later during the first half of 1878, however, an average of 418
Walthamstow residents were collecting outdoor relief from the guardians of the West
Ham Poor Law Union, at a weekly cost to Walthamstow ratepayers of £25 10s. 2d.,
far more than in the neighbouring parish of Leyton, where there were no parochial
charities.[3] During the following year that number had increased even further to 517
Walthamstow residents and their dependents receiving outdoor relief.[4] In Walthamstow
the poor rates, which had dropped dramatically from 60d. in the pound after the
creation of the West Ham Poor Law Union in 1836, had begun to creep upwards again
from 24d. in the pound in the 1840s to almost double that rate in the 1870s.[5] Ratepayers, searching for their own relief, focused on the funds of the parochial charities.

     In addition to their concern about rising poor rates, Walthamstow ratepayers
were also concerned about schools. By the mid-1870s the Sir George Monoux School,
funded by the charities of George Monoux and Henry Maynard, had fallen on hard
times. Mr. Griggs, master of the school for the past thirty years, described the Monoux
schoolroom as dark, badly ventilated, dirty, and dilapidated. Although the room could
accommodate 70 pupils, there were only 40 desks and only 12 boys between the ages

of 7 and 14, children of tradesmen and clerks, currently attending the school, where
they were taught reading, writing, arithmetic, geography, and mathematics.[6] Other
Walthamstow schools, including a National School for 410 boys, a National School
for 330 girls, three British schools at Wood Street, Marsh Street, and Higham Hill, and
a number of Church of England Schools, provided primary education for most
Walthamstow children, but the nearest grammar school was the Grocers' Company's
School at Hackney Downs in Clapton.[7] The fees charged by such grammar schools,
however, placed them beyond the reach of labouring workmen, tradesmen, and even
most city clerks.

This lack of a grammar school education for children of the growing middle
class was not confined to Walthamstow. To encourage the building and endowment of
new schools, The Endowed Schools Act 1869 had permitted the Endowed Schools
Commissioners, with the consent of the trustees of any charitable endowment, to
divert funds from other charitable purposes, including 'doles in money or kind', to the
advancement of education. Following an application by William Houghton on behalf
of the Monoux Charity, William Latham, Assistant Commissioner of the Endowed
Schools Commission, wrote on 4 December 1871 proposing re-organisation of the
funding of education in Walthamstow. A grammar school accommodating 200 boys
would require a capital outlay of £5,000 for a site, new school buildings, master's
house, and some permanent endowment for the provision of scholarships, prizes, and
maintenance. Pointing out that the strictly educational endowments at Walthamstow
arising from the gifts of George Monoux and Henry Maynard consisted of indifferent
school buildings and an annual income of only £50 2s. 10d., and that the value of
stock held by all the Walthamstow charities exceeded £6,000, Latham invited Houghton
and the parishioners of Walthamstow to consider how much, if any, they might be
willing to divert from poor relief to education.[8] Draft schemes for the re-organisation
of the Sir George Monoux School and the Henry Maynard Charity were published in
February 1873, but controversy over whether or not the school should be non-sectarian
had sidelined the reform.

At a meeting of the Walthamstow Vestry on 24 April 1876, the issue surfaced
again. At the instigation of James Higham, the Vestry appointed a committee to
investigate the terms and management of the Walthamstow charities. Later that year
Vestry clerk William Houghton submitted to a public Vestry meeting a detailed summary
of the assets and conditions of each charity, which was printed in 1877 under the title
'An Account of Benefactions in the Parish of St Mary, Walthamstow, in the County
of Essex, Extracted from the Original Instruments, and Printed by Order of Vestry,
held on 25th August, 1876'. Five hundred copies were ordered to be printed at
charity expense and made available to ratepayers for the small charge of sixpence.
By Houghton's calculation the annual income of the 37 charities amounted to
£1,166 7s. 11d. to be distributed according to the wishes of the donors for education,
apprenticeships, relief of poverty, maintenance of family monuments, and support of
the vicar and parish officers.[9] Further meetings of the vestry committee led to another

visit on 16 October by the Endowed Schools Commissioner William Latham, who suggested a formal inquiry by the Charity Commission to consider which charities might be diverted for the purposes of education.

Higham, in a letter published in *The Walthamstow Guardian* on 14 October 1876, had taken it upon himself to invite the public to attend this meeting, thus ensuring that the subject would be throughly discussed in the leader columns and letter pages of the local press. On 21 October *The Walthamstow Guardian* obligingly ran a lengthy account of the meeting and in its editorial argued, 'In the matter of these charities, far be it from us to wish to take the coals and the bread from those who need and deserve them—but why should these emblems of charity be the only way in which these legacies are dispensed.'[10] Public opinion was aroused. Some people argued that part of the oversubscribed dole charities should be used to provide a first class grammar school to which able children of the poorer classes would have access by scholarships and children of the middle classes by payment of fees. Others maintained that charity trustees must honour the wishes of charitable benefactors and not use charitable money for any purpose other than that for which it had been given. Still others supported the provision of education, but thought funds could be found elsewhere.

The Charity Commission inquiry into the Walthamstow charities began on 20 November 1876 in the Public Hall, Orford Road, before Inspector William Good and concluded its initial phase on 2 December. Reported in detail by the press, the inquiry reviewed the terms, assets, and income of each charity and urged the Vestry committee and others attending to consider the re-organisation of the management of the charities.[11] After adjourning to study his findings, Inspector Good resumed the inquiry on 14 March 1877, focusing this time on the details of the proposed new governing body and the diversion of funds for a new grammar school.[12] Although Inspector Good made it clear that the impetus for change must come through formal application from the trustees of each charity, during the course of the inquiry he made his own views amply clear: the administration of the charities should be streamlined under one board of management; financial accounting must be standardised; trustees not resident in Walthamstow should be disqualified from serving; since the poorest residents were cared for by outdoor relief from the board of guardians of the West Ham Poor Law Union, the number of Walthamstow residents now needing doles of bread and coal was limited; in contrast, since Walthamstow did need a grammar school, funds should be diverted from poor relief for that purpose.

Not all the trustees of the various Walthamstow charities were prepared to join in a formal application for the proposed new scheme to amalgamate the parish charities under a central board. The Rev. Thomas Parry, vicar of St Mary's, led the opposition. Fearing, for example, that new governors would disregard Mary Squire's intention that her six almswomen be members of the Church of England, he objected to the transfer of the Squire's Almshouses to an amalgamated charity board; and for the same reason he objected to the transfer of Mary Newell's Charity, which sponsored apprenticeships for boys whose parents belonged to the Established Church. On the subject of diverting charity funds from poor relief to education, the vicar had been quoted in the press as saying, 'he was not willing to alienate any charity which specially belonged to the poor for any purpose of education' and that 'he could not consent to give his willing approval to any property being diverted from the really poor and given for educational purposes, and to a class for whom it had not been intended'.[13]

Some of the trustees, however, were prepared to act. After applications from the overseers and churchwardens dated 19 September 1879 and from the Monoux trustees dated 9 December 1879, the Charity Commission eventually produced a draft Scheme proposing a new governing body to be known as the Walthamstow Charity Governors, comprising the vicar and churchwardens as ex-officio governors, six representative governors each serving a term of three years to be appointed by the Vestry from the resident ratepayers of Walthamstow, and four co-optative governors each serving a term of five years to be chosen in the first instance by the Charity Commission and thereafter by the Charity Governors. All land and shares were to be vested in The Official Trustee of Charity Lands or the Official Trustee of Charitable Funds. The Vestry approved the draft scheme with the addition of the overseers as ex-officio members, making a governing body of fifteen.

In the end the new Charity Commission Scheme sealed on 30 April 1880 amalgamated the 11 charities of Robert Rampston, Thomas Colby, Richard Garnett, Anthony Compton and Thomas Turner, Sigismund Trafford, Jeremiah Wakelin, Thomas Legendre, Catherine Woolball, Thomas Sims, John Rigge, and John Morley—all controlled by vicar and churchwardens—and the five charities of George Monoux, Richard Banks, John Harman, William Bedford, and Elizabeth Collard—controlled by William Houghton, David Thomas Morgan, Thomas Naunton Cuffley, Eliot Howard, Edward Twining, John Evennett, Henry Collier, William Sims Horner, Alfred Turner, Benjamin Michael Tite, Francis Wragg, and the churchwardens George Samuel Pritchard and Robert Flexman Budd. Together these charities represented assets of £4,387 10s. 3d. in shares, £15 in rentcharges, 15a.1r. 25p. in land and premises including Vestry House and the Monoux almshouses.[14] The first accounts to the Charity Commission for the year ending 30 April 1881 showed receipts of £210 17s. 4d., expenditure of £175 3s. 7d., and a balance of £35 13s. 9d.[15]

The first co-optative governors appointed by the scheme for a term of five years were Eliot Howard, hydraulic engineer, David Thomas Morgan, merchant, William Sims Horner, builder, and John Francis Holcombe Read. The election of the representative governors took place between 18 and 21 June 1880 with nine candidates standing for six places. In the event six candidates—all familiar names on the Walthamstow Vestry— Ebenezer Clarke, Thomas Naunton Cuffley, merchant, David Howard, JP, James Higham, Edward Twining, surgeon, and William Elliott Whittingham, merchant—were elected by a wide margin and took their place along with the ex-officio overseers and the churchwardens George Samuel Pritchard, builder, and Robert Flexman Budd, corn merchant.[16] William Houghton, solicitor, was appointed as Clerk to the Governors, and the Rev. Thomas Parry was chosen as chairman.

At first little had changed either in the choice of charity governors or in the distribution of charity income. Pending a further scheme, the Charity Commissioners had ordered that the 'net yearly income of the Charities shall be applied by the Governors in accordance with the trusts declared respecting the same Charities respectively by the several founders thereof'.[17] Further Charity Commission schemes, however, soon radically strengthened the position of the Walthamstow Charity Governors. The Monoux School had closed in 1878, following the death of the schoolmaster Mr. Griggs, and control of the school had passed to the Charity Governors in 1880. On 9 September 1884 the Charity Commission issued a scheme for the refoundation of the Monoux School, appropriating under Section 30 of The Endowed Schools Act 1869 the sums of £130 of the annual income of the Inhabitants' Donation Trust and £50 of Wise's Gift to supplement the educational income provided by the Monoux Charity and Maynard Charity. The Walthamstow Charity Governors were directed to serve as school governors. A school was to be built 'suitable for not less than two hundred day scholars' and a headmaster appointed who 'shall be a graduate of some University in the United Kingdom' at a yearly salary of £100. Boys would pay tuition to be fixed between £3 and £6 a year, and not less than twenty free scholarships were to be offered to deserving poor boys. The curriculum was to include 'religious instruction in accordance with the principles of the Christian Faith, Reading, Writing, and Arithmetic; Geography and History; English Grammar, Composition, and Literature; Mathematics; Latin; At least one Modern Foreign European Language; Natural Science; Drawing, Drill, and Vocal Music'.[18] Re-opened in the Trinity Schoolroom on West Avenue on 14 January 1886, the Sir George Monoux School eventually moved to permanent premises in the High Street in December 1889. To pay for the new school building, a Charity Commission Scheme dated 19 May 1890 authorised the school governors to use some £3,600 of assets from seven parochial charities in exchange for a perpetual annuity of £108 paid annually to

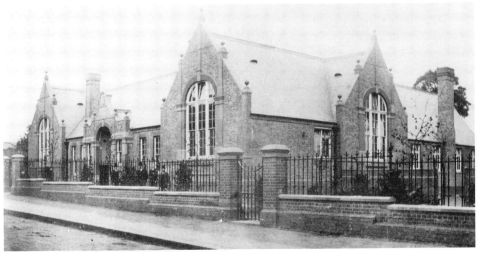

39 Sir George Monoux School on the High Street.

the Charity Governors.[19] On 16 April 1886 the Charity Commission also sealed a scheme discharging the trustees of Sir Henry Maynard's Charity and vesting in the Walthamstow Charity Governors the land containing 51 acres at Higham Hill known as Bull's Farm and the land containing 30 acres at Hale End known as Stretman's Farm and a sum of £514 13s. 3d. invested in annuities.[20]

During the early 1890s, then, the Walthamstow charities were controlled by four principal sets of trustees.[21] Statements of Accounts for the year ending 30 April 1890 show that the Walthamstow Charity Governors now controlled 18 charities with total receipts of £398 7s. and total payments of £385 17s. 1d., including monthly stipends to Monoux almsfolk of 11s. each. In addition they accounted for £382 3s. 4d. income from the Maynard Charity, part of which was transferred to the vicar and church-wardens. The churchwardens Edwin Knott and Francis Mercer still accounted for the receipts of the charities of Hyll, Conyers, Gamuel, the Inhabitants Donation, Corbett, Wise, Holbrook, Cass, Cluff, Newell, and the churchwardens' share of the Maynard Charity, amounting in all to £836 19s. 2d. during the year ending 30 April 1890. Accounts of the Charity of Jane Sabina Collard, administered by trustees William Houghton, William Elliott Whittingham, and Gilbert Houghton, show receipts that same year of £186 10s. 5d. and payments of £180 10s. 1d. including monthly stipends

40   Monument of the Rev. Thomas Parry.

of 16s. to each of 10 almsfolk in the Collard Almshouses. Finally, the vicar, the Rev. Thomas Parry, controlled the Mary Squire Almshouses and the related chari-ties of Elizabeth Collard, which contrib-uted to the stipends of the six widows, and Mary Cox, which contributed to the repairs of the almshouses. Two years later, following the death of the Rev. Thomas Parry on 29 January 1892 and the appoint-ment of the Rev. William Langhorne as vicar of St Mary's, the administration of the Squire's Almshouses and the related charities of Elizabeth Collard and Mary Cox passed into the hands of the Walthamstow Charity Governors. Aside from that change, however, charity affairs might have continued in this state for some years to come, if it had not been for James Joseph McSheedy and yet another Charity Commission inquiry.

Radical Irish politician and Liberal reformer who settled in Walthamstow while working for the London School

Board, James McSheedy became headmaster of Winns Avenue School and in the words of *The Walthamstow Guardian* 'soon became the storm centre of the public life of the district'. The battle centred on the demand for a more democratic system of parochial voting; the chosen battleground centred on the parochial charities. Years later, looking back over McSheedy's career, *The Walthamstow Guardian* wrote in his obituary:

> The battle of the charities was largely fought out in the vestry meeting, which, instead of being the arena for theological disputants, was the venue where parochial and civic affairs were warmly discussed. The radical reformers claimed that the charities were not efficiently administered and that they were largely given to those who were members or adherents of the national church. Long and stormy were the meetings presided over by the Rev. Thomas Parry and his successor, Mr. Langhorne. On occasions the vestry, adjourned from time to time, spread over nearly a year, and the dispute between the advocates of the old order and the new sometimes got beyond heated speech, and on one occasion a decanter was hurled at the head of the redoubtable 'Mac.' Mr. McSheedy undoubtedly forced the pace with regard to the charities, and was mainly responsible for bringing about the Government inquiry that resulted in a scheme placing the election of trustees on a more democratic basis.[22]

Although democracy was steadily gaining ground, during the latter quarter of the 19th century Walthamstow was still ruled by oligarchy. Historically, Walthamstow had been governed by a Select Vestry consisting of the vicar, churchwardens and 18 parishioners. Whenever vacancies occurred, the Vestry had been empowered to choose 'such other parishioners of the same parish of the better sort as be grave and honest men fit for the same place'.[23] The Rev. Edmund Chishull had changed the Select Vestry to an Open Vestry early in the 18th century, but vestry meetings had still been dominated by the select few during the 18th and 19th centuries through a voting system that favoured wealthy property owners. In 1873 the secular functions of the Vestry were transferred to the democratically-elected Local Board, but the franchise for voting in Local Board elections was high with only people owning or occupying property having an annual rental value of £12 or higher able to vote. The same small group of public-minded men served as churchwardens and overseers, sat on the Vestry, the Local Board, and other public bodies, and made the decisions that affected the majority of Walthamstow residents. The solicitor William Houghton, to cite just one example, held numerous public offices, including Clerk to the Vestry, Clerk to the Church-wardens, Clerk to the Local Board, Clerk to the Burial Board, Clerk to the Walthamstow Charity Governors, Clerk to the Monoux School Governors, and Trustee and Clerk to the Jane Sabina Collard Charity. This, then, was the oligarchy assaulted in McSheedy's charges against the Walthamstow charities.

At a public Vestry meeting on 14 August 1890, convened to accept the annual charity accounts for the year ending 30 April 1890, McSheedy orchestrated the appointment of a committee chaired by himself to examine the accounts and to report back to a future Vestry.[24] At an adjourned public Vestry meeting running for three

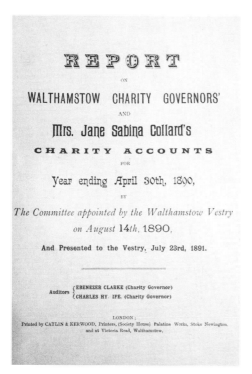

41 Report by James McSheedy on the Walthamstow Charities.

nights from 22 to 24 July 1891, McSheedy presented the committee's report, which was subsequently printed and reported extensively in the press. Consisting of a sustained attack on the churchwardens and Charity Governors, McSheedy alleged numerous instances of incorrect accounting, diversion of funds, and failure of trustees to carry out their charitable trusts, and claimed that 'the accounts were incomplete, inaccurate and deceptive, and disclosed an indefensible disregard for the rights and privileges of the poor.' Re-opening the issue of diversion of charitable dole funds to education, McSheedy attacked the Monoux School Charity Commission schemes of 19 September 1884 and 9 May 1890, charging that £4,000 had 'been taken from the poor of Walthamstow to build Monoux School'. The Vestry meetings had ended in uproar with McSheedy and his committee vowing to request a Charity Commission inquiry, an invitation that the Commissioners initially declined.[25]

Undeterred, McSheedy stepped up his attack on the Charity Governors and the Walthamstow civic oligarchy in general and William Houghton in particular during the autumn of 1891. Alleging that William Houghton and the Houghton law firm had benefited unduly at the expense of the poor of Walthamstow, McSheedy tabled a resolution to dismiss William Houghton as Clerk to the Vestry. A Vestry meeting called for that purpose on 27 October descended to disorder. Shouting and interruptions prevented speakers from being heard, and when an attempt was made to put the resolution to a vote, William Sims Horner called for a poll, which was scheduled for the following Saturday, 31 October, from 10 o'clock in the morning to 10 in the evening. Campaign literatures circulated on both sides: 'Dismissal of William Houghton: To the Working Men of Walthamstow' listing the local government activities of the Houghtons and the money received in fees; 'Mr William Houghton's Reply to Mr McSheedy's Charges'; and 'To the Ratepayers of Walthamstow' containing some 250 names with 'many other names to hand too late to include in the list' urging people to vote against McSheedy's resolution. On polling day 2,340 ratepayers recorded their votes in the Town Hall, giving William Houghton a resounding majority of 702.[26]

Unwilling and literally unable to defend themselves at the increasingly vocal and disorderly Vestry meetings, the Walthamstow Charity Governors themselves finally requested the Charity Commission to intervene and hold an inquiry. Held in the Town Hall before Mr. Edward Bouverie, barrister and Assistant Commissioner of the Charity Commission, the inquiry sat from 8 February to 17 February 1892. The previously published charges of James McSheedy were fully rehearsed, and counsel for the church-wardens and charity governors made a point-by-point defence.[25] No new evidence was advanced in support of the charges, and by the end of the proceedings little of substance remained of the accusations of McSheedy and his Committee of Inquiry.

Nevertheless, McSheedy had made his point for greater public accountability of the parochial charities, and throughout the proceedings the Commissioner had urged the participants to put forward positive proposals for the management and distribution of charity funds. McSheedy advocated a Charity Board composed of four members appointed by the Charity Commission and eleven members directly elected by a ballot of all ratepayers and directly accountable to the people of the district. Outlining his plan to the inquiry, McSheedy argued:

> Let them do away with the vicar in connection with the charities. The old vicar was dead, and he hoped the new one would not have anything to do with the charities. The Churchwardens also should not have anything to do with the charities. When he told them that the charities of Walthamstow amounted to about £2,000 a year to be distributed, with a great probability of being increased, owing to the increased population and development of Walthamstow, they would see the necessity of having a Board specially elected by the people and a Board in which the people would have confidence as to the distribution of these large charities.[28]

Declining to offer any proposal until they had been publicly vindicated of all mishandling of charitable funds, the Walthamstow Charity Governors and church-wardens eventually lodged a formal application on 28 February 1893 for a new scheme that would amalgamate all of the remaining parochial charities and transfer the selection of the representative charity governors from election by the Vestry to nomination by the Local Board with two governors representing each of the four wards into which the town had been recently divided: Hoe Street Ward, Wood Street Ward, St James Ward, and the Northern Ward. On 25 April 1894 the three trustees of the Jane Sabina Collard Charity joined in support of this application, leading eventually to a new Charity Commission Scheme sealed on 4 October 1895 creating the Walthamstow Parochial Charities.[29]

Ten

———❦———

Walthamstow Parochial Charities

THE CHARITY COMMISSION SCHEME of 4 October 1895 creating the Walthamstow Parochial Charities struck a compromise between the radical proposals of James McSheedy and the conservative response of the Walthamstow Charity Governors. There would be 10 representative trustees, not directly elected but appointed for four-year terms, eight by the recently established Walthamstow Urban District Council and two by the Guardians of the Poor representing the Parish of Walthamstow in the West Ham Poor Law Union. Of the trustees appointed by the district council, two would be residents or ratepayers in the St James Street Ward, two in the Hoe Street Ward, two in the High Street Ward, one in the Wood Street Ward, and one in the Northern Ward. Councillors for each ward would nominate the trustee or trustees, who need not be members of the council, to represent each ward, thus ensuring broadly-based representation. Trustees appointed by the poor law guardians could be residents or ratepayers anywhere in the parish. As McSheedy had proposed, there would be four co-optative trustees appointed in the first instance by the Charity Commission for seven-year terms and thereafter elected by the trustees for five-year terms. Contrary to McSheedy's suggestion, however, the vicar would serve as an ex-officio trustee, maintaining the connection between the charities and the church and making up the total of 15 trustees.[1] In 1908 the scheme was varied to end the appointment of trustees by the poor law guardians and to increase the appointment by the Urban District Council to two trustees from the Wood Street Ward and two from the Northern Ward.[2] In 1914, following the division of the Northern Ward into Hale End Ward and Higham Hill Ward, the Scheme was amended again to provide for the appointment of two trustees from each ward, making a total of 17 trustees.[3]

The first co-optative trustees chosen by the Charity Commission were Eliot Howard, the Rev. Frederic John Poole, William McCall, and William Elliott

42 Charity Commission Scheme for the Walthamstow Parochial Charities, 4 October 1895.

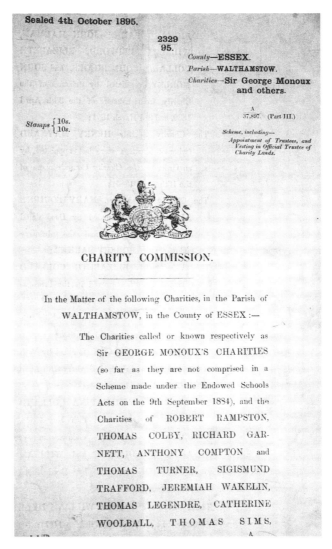

Sealed 4th October 1895.

2329
95.

County—**ESSEX**.

Parish—**WALTHAMSTOW**.

Charities—**Sir George Monoux and others.**

A
37,897. (Part III.)

Scheme, including—

Appointment of Trustees, and Vesting in Official Trustee of Charity Lands.

Stamps { 10s.
{ 10s.

CHARITY COMMISSION.

In the Matter of the following Charities, in the Parish of

WALTHAMSTOW, in the County of ESSEX :—

The Charities called or known respectively as

Sir GEORGE MONOUX'S CHARITIES

(so far as they are not comprised in a

Scheme made under the Endowed Schools

Acts on the 9th September 1884), and the

Charities of ROBERT RAMPSTON,

THOMAS COLBY, RICHARD GAR-

NETT, ANTHONY COMPTON and

THOMAS TURNER, SIGISMUND

TRAFFORD, JEREMIAH WAKELIN,

THOMAS LEGENDRE, CATHERINE

WOOLBALL, T H O M A S S I M S,

A

Whittingham. Representative trustees included Ebenezer Clarke and William Gower from Hoe Street Ward, William Beck from Wood Street Ward, Walter Thompson from the Northern Ward, and John Anderson and James McSheedy from St James Street Ward. Only five of the old Walthamstow Charity Governors continued as trustees of the new Walthamstow Parochial Charities, thus guaranteeing a fresh start for the Walthamstow charities.

New directions were also established for the application of charity income. Aside from maintaining the Sir George Monoux Almshouses and paying stipends to the almsfolk, the Walthamstow Charity Governors had made general distributions of bread and coals to the poor throughout the parish. During the year from Easter 1881 to Easter 1882, for example, the charity governors had paid monthly stipends

No. 243

Walthamstow Charity Governors.

BREAD TICKET

To the Value of Three Shillings.

Please to supply to Mr._____Bread
of good quality at the lowest price, to the above value,
as required, and send in your account with the vouchers,
to Mr. Ebenezer Clarke, Grove Road, not later than
15th February, 1895.

TOWN HALL,   W. HOUGHTON,
    WALTHAMSTOW.   *Clerk to the Governors*

*The Tradesman Supplying the Bread is requested to write
his name and address on the back of the card.*

43 Bread ticket issued by
the Walthamstow Charity
Governors.

to the Monoux almsfolk of 11s. each, additional annual gifts to each almsperson on
St Bartholomew's Day, St Thomas' Day, and Ash Wednesday amounting in total to
14s. 1d. in money and 16s. in coal, and from the Charity of Elizabeth Collard a
further annual stipend of 8s. 4d. The other major expenditure for the Charity
Governors that year amounted to £40 in New Year's gifts distributed to 160 people,
each receiving 3s. in bread and 2s. in coal.[4] The application forms for these New
Year's gifts had to be countersigned by 'a respectable Householder' certifying the
applicant as 'a deserving case'. Questions included 'How long resident in
Walthamstow?', 'Are you a Widow or Widower?', 'How many children have you
dependent on you for support?', and 'How much do you earn per week?' Most of
the accounts of the Walthamstow Charity Governors have been lost, but for the 1889
distribution 348 such applications survive; for 1894, 148 applications; and for 1895,
211 applications.[5] Successful applicants were given bread tickets and coal tickets
to be redeemed by local merchants.[6] During the same year the churchwardens, from
the charity income under their control, paid additional monthly stipends of
5s. each to the Monoux almsfolk, monthly stipends of 10s. each to 20 poor
widows, and almost £280 in general distribution of bread and coal to recipients
recommended by the ministers of the churches and chapels throughout the town.
Like the Charity Governors, the churchwardens used the ticket system, making distributions each Sunday at the church doors of St Mary's, St Saviour's, St John's, and
St Peter's.[7]

Under the new scheme, however, application of income by the trustees of the
Walthamstow Parochial Charities moved away from the weekly direct distribution of
bread and coal. With three sets of almshouses now under their control, the primary
objective of the trustees became the maintenance of the almspeople: eight men and
five women in the Sir George Monoux Almshouses, 'six widows of tradesmen of the
Parish of Walthamstow, being members of the Church of England, with a preference

for those who have become reduced by misfortune from better circumstances' in the Mary Squire's Almshouses, and 10 men 'over sixty years of age who have not at any time been engaged or employed in domestic service, or received Poor-law relief' in the Jane Sabina Collard Almshouses. All the almspeople were to be

> poor persons of good character, who have resided in the Parish of Walthamstow for not less than five years next preceding the time of their appointment, who have not during that period received Poor-law relief, and who from age, ill-health, accident, or infirmity, are unable to maintain themselves by their own exertions.

In addition to paying the almspeople weekly stipends of 5s., the trustees were authorised by the scheme to appoint 'a Medical Officer to attend upon the Almspeople, and to supply them with medicines and such medical appliances as may be necessary at a yearly salary not exceeding £40, inclusive of the cost of such medicines and appliances'.

After meeting their primary obligation to the almspeople and repairing the almshouses as necessary, the trustees of the Walthamstow Parochial Charities were authorised to apply the residue of their annual income under three general categories: the maintenance of pensioners, the 'establishment of a Hospital or Dispensary for the benefit of the poor of the Parish of Walthamstow', or making donations 'for the benefit either of the poor of the said Parish of Walthamstow generally, or of such deserving and necessitous persons resident therein as the Trustees shall select'. Since the schedule of property and investments in the 1895 scheme shows total gross yearly income of £1,709 8s., the trustees had ample resources to develop charitable programmes under all three of these categories.

First came a programme of old age pensions. Subject to the same general conditions for the appointment of almspeople and paid the same weekly stipend of 5s., pensioners were appointed upon recommendation of the trustees in each ward for a term of three years, which could then be renewed. The Walthamstow Parochial Charities Register of Pensioners reveals that the first group of 24 pensioners was appointed on 7 May 1896 with the addition of 10 more on 1 October that year and a further 10 on 17 December. Interestingly, the occupations listed in that first group for the men included hat presser, rat destroyer, ticket writer, boot-lace maker, carpenter, gardener, plumber, bricklayer, early morning caller, umbrella maker, and warehouseman (blind), and for the women widow, spinster, dressmaker, laundress, and nurse.[8] Whenever vacancies occurred, trustees advertised in the newspaper for the appointment of new pensioners. Well before the Old Age Pensions Act 1908 established a national pension of 1s. to 5s. a week given at age 70, subject to a means test, the Walthamstow Parochial Charities was providing needy old age pensioners in Walthamstow with the maximum pension established 12 years later by the Government. Nationwide, by the end of March 1909 some 500,000 people were receiving old age pensions from the state, a development which led to the amendment in the 1914 Scheme ordering that stipends for pensioners paid by the trustees 'be not less than 5s. a week including assistance received from other sources'.[9]

44 Walthamstow Parochial Charities register of pensioners.

A major boost to the pensions programme of the Walthamstow Parochial Charities came on 28 March 1924, when the Charity Commission established the Charity of Thomas Worton. Among other bequests Worton had left a sum of £30,208 16s. 4d. in shares to be administered by the Walthamstow Parochial Charities chiefly for the purpose of providing pensions for

> poor persons of good character, who (except in special cases to be approved by the Charity Commissioners) have resided in the Parish of Walthamstow for not less than five years next preceeding the time of their appointment, who are not at the time of their appointment in receipt of Poor-law relief other than medical relief, and who from age, ill-health, accident, or infirmity, are, wholly or in part, unable to maintain themselves by their own exertions.[10]

Pensions were to vary between 5s. and 15s. per week with vacancies to be advertised and applicants to be appointed by trustees in the same manner as for the existing pensioners. The Register of Pensioners for the Thomas Worton Charity reveals that between twenty and seventy pensioners each received pensions of 5s. a week at any one time between 1924 and 1962, when the last pensioners were appointed.[11]

When these additional pensions provided by the Charity of Thomas Worton were added to the general pensions provided by the 1895 scheme, in many years more than one hundred poor people received pensions from the Walthamstow Parochial Charities in addition to their basic state pensions. Neither the state pensions nor the pensions paid by the trustees were subject to the stigma of poor relief, and the stipends paid by the trustees to almspeople and pensioners prevented many poor people in reduced circumstances from having to receive outdoor relief from the Guardians of the Poor or having to enter the workhouse of the West Ham Poor Law Union. Both pensioners and almspeople, in fact, were specifically barred by the 1895 scheme from receiving poor law relief, although the 1914 scheme did allow pensioners and almspeople to receive medical relief as long as they did not enter a poor law institution.

The second general category in the 1895 scheme for the distribution of the residual income of the Walthamstow Parochial Charities was the 'establishment of a Hospital or Dispensary for the benefit of the poor of the Parish of Walthamstow.' Although the trustees did not directly develop a charitable programme in this field, during the first half of the 20th century they did come to administer several additional charities providing medical relief for the poor of Walthamstow. As well as providing pensions for the poor, the Charity of Thomas Worton in 1924 had left the sum of £7,812 10s. in shares to the Walthamstow, Wanstead and Leyton Children's and General Hospital for erecting and equipping a ward of 10 beds 'for the exclusive use of the poor of Walthamstow'. Although that bequest was not administered by the Walthamstow Parochial Charities, Worton did specify that £200 of the income from the £30,208 16s. 4d. in shares left to the Trustees of the Walthamstow Parochial Charities be spent yearly 'in contributions to Hospitals, Convalescent Homes, Dispensaries, Infirmaries, or other Charitable Institutions' (this clause was modified by a Charity Commission Scheme dated 7 March 1952 to leave the sum to the discretion of the trustees).[12]

Less than a year later, on 3 January 1925, Thomas Sutcliffe Armstrong, Walter Warrington, Herbert Arthur Muddiman, Alfred Henry McNeil, Walter Tarry Hickman and Charles Watkins, Trustees of the Hale End District Association Charity, created by a Declaration of Trust the Hale End District Association Hospital Charity with an investment of £1,020 to be administered by the Trustees of Walthamstow Parochial Charities 'for the benefit of the children of men who are serving or have served in His Majesty's Forces', and 'for the benefit of the children of deserving poor persons generally' who are resident in the Ecclesiastical District of All Saints, Higham's Park in Hale End. A fund was to be established with the Brookfield Orthopaedic Hospital at Hale End, and if that instution became funded by the state, then the fund was to be transferred to the Walthamstow Wanstead and Leyton Children's and General Hospital on Orford Road.[13] By 1952 this fund had accumulated assets of £1,754 15s. 5d., prompting the Charity Commission to rename the charity The Hale End District Association Sick Children's Fund and to broaden the application of income to

> the benefit of sick children of deserving poor persons resident in the ecclesiastical Parish of All Saints, Higham's Park, Hale End, and subject thereto for the benefit of sick poor adults resident as aforesaid in ... supply of special food and medicines, medical comforts, extra bedding, fuel and medical and surgical appliances, provision of domestic help ... or money ... to enable the recipients to obtain such benefits as aforesaid or to defray the expenses of convalescence.[14]

On 8 March 1955 the Walthamstow Parochial Charities assumed adminstration of yet another medical charity, when the Charity Commission established the

Walthamstow Sick Poor Fund from the assets of the old Walthamstow Dispensary. Assets, consisting of the house at 105 Hoe Street, £793 4s. 3d. in shares, and bank deposits of £1,935 16s. 11d., were to be applied 'for the benefit either of the sick poor of the Borough of Walthamstow generally' or in particular for 1) bedding, comforts, food, fuel and medical aids; 2) the expense of recuperative holidays or obtaining domestic help; 3) a convalescent home or organization for the benefit of the sick poor of the borough, or 4) a nurse to attend the almspeople of the Walthamstow Parochial Charities.[15]

The third general category in the 1895 scheme for the distribution of residual income was contributions or donations for the following purposes: for a dispensary, infirmary, hospital or convalescent home 'in which children suffering from any bodily infirmity are taught any trade or employment'; for a 'Provident Club or Society established in Walthamstow for the supply of Coal, Clothing, or other necessaries'; for the provision of nurses or for traveling expenses of patients; for 'the cost of the Outfit, on entering upon a trade or occupation, or into service, of any person under the age of 21 years'; for passage money in aid of emigration of any person; and for supply of temporary relief 'in cases of unexpected loss, or sudden destitution'. Although the survival of blank application forms for recommendations to the Children's Shoe Committee in 1884 and a bill for 23 pairs of girls' boots in 1889 suggest some general distribution of clothing by the old Walthamstow Charity Governors,[16] the principal programme under the heading of donations developed by the Walthamstow Parochial Charities was the distribution of coal.

45   Applications for coal vouchers issued by the Walthamstow Charity Governors.

Coal distribution to the poor had a long history in Walthamstow, beginning with the Charity of George Monoux, which had specified the annual delivery of £5 in coal to his almspeople during the months of November, December, January, and February.[17] In 1752, Thomas Legendre had left £600 so that 'within ffourteen days before Christmas Shall be delivered to each poor person no less than two Sacks and not more than three Sacks of Coals forever'.[18] In 1796 Mary Squire, in addition to establishing her almshouses, had left money for the purchasing and distributing of 'such coals as equally as might be among twelve poor Housekeepers of the said parish of Walthamstow who should not be inhabitants of any almshouses in the said parish'.[19] In 1874, William Cluff had left a legacy of £1,000, the dividends from which were to be 'applied every Christmas in giving to thirty poor deserving people living in the said Parish of Walthamstow five sacks of good Coals each'.[20] More recently, in 1924 Thomas Worton had directed that £50 from his legacy be paid yearly for donations to 'any Provident Club or Society established in Walthamstow for the supply of Coal, Clothing or other necessaries'.[21]

Following the establishment of the 1895 Scheme, the trustees of the Walthamstow Parochial Charities continued this long tradition of coal distribution, simply adapting the procedure to fit their new administrative structure. Each year in September or October a newpaper advertisement announced that 'the Trustees will distribute during the two weeks preceding Christmas to a number of poor deserving people in the Borough Five cwts. of Coal each'.[22] Application forms were distributed and collected by the Clerk to the Trustees and considered in the November meeting of the trustees, with the representative trustees from each ward vetting the applications.

Another charitable programme with a long tradition in Walthamstow was the provision of allotments for the poor and for Walthamstow residents generally. The 1895 scheme gave the charity trustees permission to set apart any of their lands to be let in allotments, leading to the establishment of the Trencherfield Allotments located on the south side of Billet Road and further allotments on both the east and west sides of Folly Lane on land belonging to the Charity of Henry Maynard, allotments at Hale End and Hale Brinks on land belonging to the Charity of Thomas Colby, and Honeybone Allotments on Markhouse Road on land belonging to the Charity of Thomas Gamuel. Allotment registers survive for Trencherfield and Folly Lane West from 1887, for Hale Brinks from 1900, for Honeybone from 1903, for Hale End from 1905, and for Folly Lane West from 1922 until the sale of that land in 1937. An allotments manager was hired to manage the properties, enforce the rules, and collect the rents.

Additional allotments belonging to The Spade Husbandry Trust also came under the administration of the Walthamstow Parochial Charities in 1941. The Spade Husbandry Trust had been founded in 1830 for the purpose of obtaining 'suitable pieces of land, to be let in allotments to the Industrious Poor for cultivation by the Spade;' and in 1834 the lord of the manor of Walthamstow Toni had agreed to grant 10 acres of waste land near Forest Road to 'four or five respectable inhabitants of the

Parish 'at an annual quit rent of a few shillings who should underlet to the labourers at moderate rents'.[23] The land had been enfranchised in 1924, and part of it had been compulsorily purchased by The Metropolitan Water Board in 1939.[24] During 1930s the Walthamstow Parochial Charities had proposed that they take over the running of the Spade Husbandry Trust; and finally in 1941 the surviving trustees, Frederick John Hitchman, Theodore Godlee and Archibald James Higham, petitioned the Charity Commission to transfer to the Walthamstow Parochial Charities the administration and assets of the Trust, which included over eight acres of land located on the south side of Forest Road; £3,179 13s. 9d. in shares, and £166 2s.1d. in cash. By a Charity Commission scheme dated 7 February 1941, the trustees of the Walthamstow Parochial Charities were directed to apply the income

> in renting at a reasonable rent land in the said Parish suitable for letting in allotments and if and so far as the Trustees are unable to apply the said income for that purpose, in the supply of clothes, boots, linen, bedding, fuel, tools, medical or other aid in sickness, food or other articles in kind, for the benefit of such poor persons resident in the said Parish and not in receipt of Poor-law relief.[25]

These were the principal charitable programmes, then, of the Walthamstow Parochial Charities throughout the first half of the 20th century: administration of allotments, distribution of coal, support of hospitals and other medical institutions, payment of stipends to pensioners and almspeople, and maintenance of the almshouses of Sir George Monoux, Mrs. Mary Squire, and Mrs. Jane Sabina Collard. Few financial records survive for the early years of the Walthamstow Parochial Charities, but the annual report for the year ending 25 December 1942 illustrates the typical application of income to these charitable programmes.[26] Payment of stipends to the almspeople that year totalled £351 12s. 6d. and pension payments of 5s. each week to approximately 110 pensioners from Thomas Worton's Charity and from the General Maintenance Fund totalled £1,429 6s. 6d. Grants to hospitals and similar institutions, mostly made from Thomas Worton's Charity and the Hale End District Association Hospital Charity, amounted to £342 16s. 8d., and small emergency grants to individuals amounted to £31 15s. The annual distribution of coal during the 1941 Christmas season amounted to £59 8s. 9d. A salary of £38 10s. was paid to the allotments manager, who collected £193 19s. in allotment rents from charity lands. Altogether the total receipts for 1942 amounted to £4,413 2s. 6d. and total payments to £4,479 12s. 10d. The trustees of the Walthamstow Parochial Charities continued to make similar charitable payments over the next fifteen years until 1957, when a new Charity Commission scheme created the Walthamstow Almshouse and General Charities.

Eleven

Walthamstow Almshouse and General Charities

T HE NEW CHARITY COMMISSION SCHEME dated 22 March 1957, unlike the earlier schemes of 1880 and 1895, brought no dramatic political changes for the Walthamstow Parochial Charities. No change occurred to the governing body of the charities; the same trustees continued to serve under the new scheme; and the minutes and accounts continued in the same books without any break. Numerous other changes just as significant, however, reflected the growth and development of the Walthamstow charities since the 1895 scheme and established the pattern for the remainder of the 20th century. First, the 1957 scheme severed the relationship between the charities and the Sir George Monoux School. In 1907, the school governors had sold to the charity trustees the master's house and the old schoolrooms extending over the Monoux Almshouses on the east and west sides of the house in exchange for an annual rentcharge of £10 paid to the school.[1] In the 1950s the charity trustees were also still making annual payments to the school of £130 from the Inhabitants Donation and £50 from the Charity of Edmund Wise as ordered by the Charity Commissioners in 1884 acting under The Endowed Schools Act 1869. In turn, the Sir George Monoux School was still paying to the charity trustees the perpetual annuities totalling £108 12s. 9d. ordered by the Charity Commissioners in 1890, when assets of the charities had been exchanged for perpetual annuities from the school governors in order to

46   Sir George Monoux School on Chingford Road.

fund the new school building. All these annual payments to and from the school and
the charities were amalgamated in the 1957 scheme into one transfer of £3,521 of
capital assets from the charities to the Sir George Monoux Grammar School
Foundation, and the two institutions became officially separate.[2] Coming under control
of the Local Education Authority in 1920, the school operated as a grammar school
for boys until 1968, as a comprehensive school until 1986, as a sixth-form college
admitting both boys and girls until 1993, and operates today on its site in Chingford
Road as an incorporated college known as the Sir George Monoux College.

The new Scheme also tidied up other administrative details. The charity trustees
were still making a number of small mandatory annual payments, specified under the
original charitable bequests, to the vicar and various church officers for the preaching
of memorial sermons and the maintenance of monuments. Many of these payments
were amalgamated into the Walthamstow Ecclesiastical Charity, and a lump capital
sum was transferred to the churchwardens of St Mary's Church.[3] Two additional
charities—the Charity of John Cossar and the Charity of Thomas Worton—which the
charity trustees had been administering for some time were also brought into the
scheme. The Charity of John Cossar, established by his Will proved on 6 July 1892,
had come into possession of the charity trustees too late for inclusion in the 1895
scheme. John Cossar, a Walthamstow carpenter, had bequeathed his house in Forest
Road to his wife Susanna and after her decease to the trustees of the Mary Squire
Almshouses, the proceeds from its sale to be applied to the maintenance and repair of
the almshouses. After her death the house was sold, and the proceeds invested in
shares by the charity trustees. In addition to this small charity, the trustees had also
been administering the major pension programme established by the Charity of Thomas
Worton in 1924. Finally, the new scheme, reflecting the position of the charity trustees
as trustees not only of the Walthamstow Parochial Charities but also of The Hale End
District Association Sick Children's Fund, The Walthamstow Sick Poor Fund, and
The Spade Husbandry Trust, renamed the collective charities the Walthamstow
Almshouse and General Charities.

In addition to these details, the 1957 scheme authorised significant changes in the
application of charity income reflecting the social changes that had taken place in post-
war Britain, changes no doubt unimaginable to the benefactors of the Walthamstow
charities who for centuries had so carefully provided for weekly stipends to the almspeople
and weekly doles of bread and coal to the poor residents of Walthamstow. The first
change related to the weekly stipends of five shillings paid since 1895 by the trustees of
the Walthamstow Parochial Charities to pensioners. The 1895 scheme had been ahead
of its time, providing for the payment of pensions years before the government introduced
the universal payment of old age pensions. The 1924 scheme had even increased the
maximum weekly stipends and pensions payable by the trustees to 15s., bringing the
pensions paid from the general fund into line with those paid from the Charity of
Thomas Worton.[4] The sweeping social changes brought about by the Beveridge Report
in 1945, however, had removed the pressing need for such allowances. The general

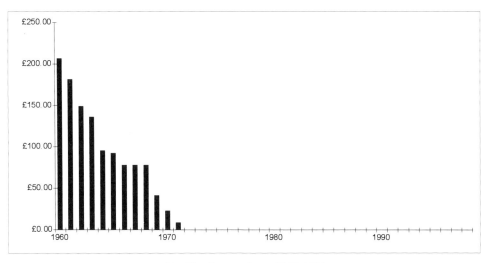

47 Charity pensions, 1960-1999.

election in July 1945 had been fought largely on the Beveridge proposals for universal social security, housing benefits and medical benefits. The Labour Government came into office pledged to carry into effect the Beveridge Plan, and it quickly raised the old age pension to 26s. a week, thus rendering largely superfluous the pensions and stipends paid by the charity trustees.[5] In fact, if a pensioner received more than 10s. 6d. a week from other sources, his state pension was reduced accordingly. The 1957 scheme permitted the continuation of weekly allowances of not more than 10s., but it encouraged the trustees to think more creatively about the application of their income, adding the proviso 'that instead of paying the whole of such weekly allowance to any recipient in money the Trustees may spend all or part thereof for his or her benefit in such ways as they think fit.' In effect, funds formerly used only for pensions could be applied for other purposes, providing they benefited 'the poor of the Borough of Walthamstow' generally or in particular 'such poor persons resident therein as the Trustees select'.[6] Following the establishment of the 1957 scheme, then, the trustees continued payments to those people currently receiving pensions, but gradually phased out the pension programme during the 1960s, the last payment being made in 1972.[7]

Even as the payment of pensions to Walthamstow residents declined and eventually ceased, the trustees extended and increased their programme of charitable donations for the general benefit of the poor of Walthamstow.[8] The annual distribution of coal to poor residents at Christmas had continued unchanged during the early 1960s. In 1965, reflecting the general adoption of central heating in residential premises, however, fuel vouchers were substituted for coal. The resulting increase in applications prompted the trustees in 1968 to limit applicants 'to poor deserving people residing in the OLD Borough of Walthamstow' and to add that 'ALL applicants must be 75 YEARS OF AGE OR OVER.'[9] Even with these restrictions, in 1983 trustees distributed 474 fuel

vouchers each worth £5, making a total distribution of £2,370. In 1987, when the
trustees increased the payment to £10, 560 fuel vouchers were distributed, making a
total of £5,600. Eventually the vetting of hundreds of applications and the distribution
of hundreds of vouchers became too cumbersome to administer. Trustees voted on
21 September 1989 to discontinue the programme of winter fuel payments and to
announce in the local press 'that the funds would now be distributed in a different way
to the elderly and inform with specific needs in the old borough of Walthamstow.'[10]

Although the trustees ended their long tradition of winter fuel payments for the
poor of Walthamstow, during the last decade of the 20th century they increased their
general programme of charitable donations both to particular individuals and to
organisations whose activities benefit Walthamstow residents generally. The 1957 scheme
had authorised trustees to make 'gifts of bedding, clothing, food, fuel, furniture or
other useful articles including comforts or other aids for the sick' and in general to
make 'gifts in money to relieve sickness, infirmity or distress'.[11] During the 1990s the
trustees have worked closely with social workers from the Department of Social Services,
Age Concern, and other similar oganisations, who have recommended particular poor
and needy individuals to the trustees for charitable grants. Having interviewed the
applicants in the presence of the social worker, trustees then make appropriate grants
to be administered through the sponsoring organisation. The 1957 scheme also
authorised trustees to make grants to 'other charitable institutions or organisations
having for their object the benefit of the poor of the said borough'. Accordingly
during the 1990s the trustees have increasingly made grants to such organisations as
the Margaret Centre based at Whipps Cross Hospital, the Waltham Forest Family
Service Unit, the Waltham Forest Volunteer Bureau, the Social Centre for the Blind,
and Christian Kitchen, whose vans distribute meals in the borough. Such grants to
organisations and to individuals sponsored by the Social Services have increased from
£766 in 1960 to a high of £33,317 in 1995.

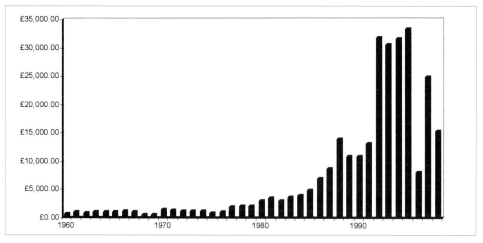

48   Charity grants, 1960-1999.

The most significant change resulting from the 1957 scheme—and the primary reason for the scheme itself—was the shift in emphasis from maintaining the almspeople to maintaining the almshouses. In 1895, the trustees of the Walthamstow Parochial Charities had inherited three sets of almshouses in various states of modernisation and repair. The Sir George Monoux Almshouses, built in 1527, had undergone extensive refurbishment in 1834. The Tudor brickwork on the external walls had been covered with a layer of modern bricks. New doors and windows had been installed, and the exposed oak timber framing on the overhanging centre gable had been covered with rough cast. A low extension to the rear of the almshouses built at the same time had provided a small kitchen and larder, but the houses had no sanitary facilities apart from a w.c. located at the end of each garden. A fireplace in the main room supplied the only heating. George Monoux had provided stipends for his almspeople, but had left little or no funds for repairs or replacement. The Mary Squire Almshouses, built in 1795, had followed much the same architectural plan: one large living room with a bed recess and a fireplace supplying the only heating. Sometime during the 19th century a low extension to the rear of each house had provided a kitchen, and a w.c. had been built at the bottom of each garden. In her Will Mary Squire had designated the sum of £3 annually for repairs, but no fund had been established and in practice all the annual income had been spent on stipends and coals.[12] Although the most modern of the three, the Jane Sabina Collard Almshouses, constructed in 1881, also lacked internal sanitary facilities. The charity did, however, have a small repair fund. A Charity Commission Scheme dated 17 February 1891 had ordered that the surplus income of the Jane Sabina Collard Charity be invested in a building fund, which in 1895 had amounted to £279 14s. 11d.[13]

The 1895 scheme had suceeded in uniting the administration of all three sets of almshouses under one board of trustees and had made ample provision for stipends to be paid to the almspeople, but except for a general clause about repairing and insuring property, it had made no provision for an extraordinary repair fund for reconstruction or improvement of the almshouses.[14] Each time major repairs were necessary to the almshouses, permission was required from the Charity Commission to borrow from other charity funds. When the roof of the Monoux Almshouses was re-tiled in 1908 and other repairs were carried out to the chimneys and brickwork requiring the expenditure of £274, for example, a Charity Commission Sealed Order had authorised the selling of stock from the Jane Sabina Collard Charity and had made provision for its replacement over the next 10 years.[15] Each repair was dealt with on a similar *ad hoc* basis, an administrative blunder pointed out with rueful hindsight by the Charity Commission in a letter dated 20 August 1954:

> At no time during this long period has the question been broached of building up a reserve normally called an extra-ordinary repair fund for these and the other Almshouses of the charities, though the stipends of the inmates were raised in 1924. More recent experience has demonstrated that no building lasts for ever, and that this aspect of Almshouse charities had been woefully neglected.[16]

49   War damage to the Sir George Monoux Almshouses.

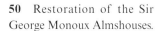

50   Restoration of the Sir George Monoux Almshouses.

This was the situation, then, on 8 October 1940, when a German bomb reduced to rubble most of the west wing of the Sir George Monoux Almshouses.

After the Second World War ended, the trustees approached George Hamilton, a retired London architect living at 16 The Drive, Walthamstow, for advice on rebuilding the Monoux Almshouses. In April 1949 Hamilton produced a plan and specification for rebuilding of almshouses 1 to 5 and restoring the old schoolroom with the projecting chimney stack gable at the west end. Each of the new almshouses would have two rooms and a low level extension containing a scullery and w.c. In addition, Hamilton proposed to add rear extensions to houses 7 to 13, to renovate the first floor of the east wing to contain three additional almshouses, and to extend the east end of the building to include on the first floor an elevated washhouse and lavatory built on arches with the roof line at the same pitch as the main building and a stairway below providing access to the three new almshouses constructed above houses 7 to 13. Hamilton developed this plan with further drawings, which were considered by the trustees during 1950, and on 29 June 1951 the Walthamstow Borough Council granted planning permission valid for a period of three years. On 21 February 1952, however, George Hamilton reluctantly withdrew from the project owing to his advanced age of 82.[17]

The trustees then turned to Darcy Braddell of Braddell & Laurence, Chartered Architects, who produced a new report on the restoration of the Monoux Almshouses on 14 July 1952. During the spring of 1953 trustees approved Braddell's plans for rebuilding of the assembly hall, a nurse's house on two storeys, and 14 almshouses each containing a bed-sitting room, kitchen and bathroom; and in October 1953 the plans were sent to the Charity Commission with the usual request to draw on the capital assets of the charities to fund the rebuilding and renovations.[18] A Restoration and Appeal Committee was formed, including representatives from the Walthamstow Antiquarian Society and the governors of the Sir George Monoux School. The War Damage Commission had agreed to pay £5,384 to rebuild the damaged portion of the west wing, and the Walthamstow Borough Council had made an Improvement Grant of £1,207 under the Housing Act 1949 to renovate houses 5 and 6. A Monoux Almshouses Reconstruction Fund was opened at Barclays Bank on Hoe Street, and plans were made for the launch in September 1954 of a Restoration Appeal to raise an additional £7,000. Meanwhile, in order to avoid the lapse of planning permission on 29 June 1954, the trustees had let the contract for the first phase of the rebuilding and modernisation programme, and in July they requested Charity Commission authorisation for an overdraft of £5,000 in order to meet the building certificates.[19]

At this point the Charity Commission responded with three requirements that dramatically altered the future course

51 Doorway of the restored Monoux Almshouses and the plaque above the doorway of the restored Almshouses.

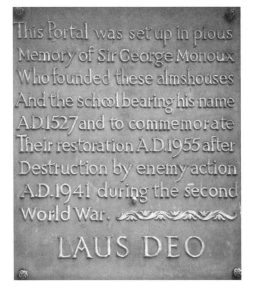

of the Walthamstow Parochial Charities. Objecting to the use of capital assets not authorised by the 1895 scheme and reacting with surprise that the project had proceeded so far without prior consultation, the Charity Commissioners agreed to provide security for the loan from Barclays Bank on the condition that the trustees agree to apply for a new Charity Commission scheme to allow them to use future income and, with approval of the Commissioners, to resort to capital assets for the restoration and improvement of any of their almshouses. Under the new scheme trustees would be required to establish, and make annual payments to, an extraordinary repair fund. Secondly, since residents would be drawing general benefit from the restored almshouses, the weekly stipends paid to almspeople would have to be discontinued. Finally, the Commissioners decreed that, 'the inmates indeed might well be required to contribute some small weekly sum in aid of the fund to be built up to repay the capital advanced and to provide for some future similar restoration and improvement'.[20] On 29 September 1954 at a meeting with the Assistant Charity Commissioner and the General Secretary of the National Association of Almshouses, the trustees accepted these three require-ments. The Restoration Appeal, launched in September 1954 and wound up in December 1955, had collected only £642 1s. 2d., less than 10 per cent of its target; however, the loan from Barclays Bank, authorised by the Charity Commission Sealed Order dated 26 November 1954, did allow the trustees to complete this first phase of the restoration and improvement of the Monoux Almshouses, while they waited for the new scheme.

Following the establishment of the new Charity Commission scheme on 22 March 1957, then, the trustees of the newly constituted Walthamstow Almshouse and General Charities carried out these three fundamental changes to their charitable programme. First of all, as required by the Commissioners, the weekly stipends to almspeople, instituted by George Monoux in 1527 and augmented by numerous other Walthamstow benefactors over the centuries, were discontinued. As with pensioners, the current

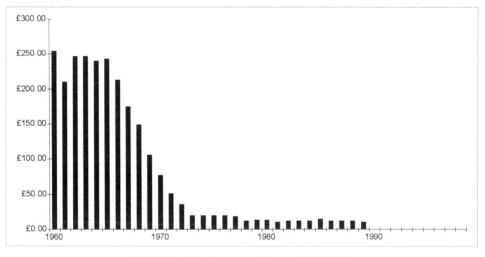

52   Stipends given to residents, 1960-1999.

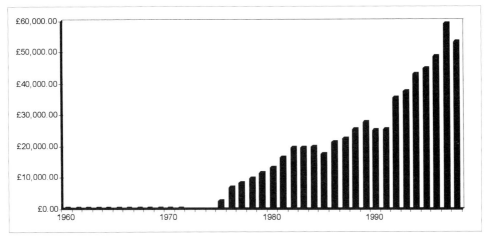

53   Contributions from the residents, 1960-1999.

almshouse residents continued to receive maximum weekly stipends of 10s., but like the pensions, stipends were gradually phased out, the last stipend being paid in 1989.[21]

The second fundamental change resulting from the 1957 scheme related to the institution of contributions by almshouse residents toward the cost of heating and maintaining the almshouses. 'The Trustees may make it a condition of appointing or permitting any person to be or remain an almsperson that he or she shall contribute towards the cost of maintaining the almshouses a weekly sum of not more than 5s. or such sum as the Charity Commissioners approve from time to time.'[22] Following this provision of the 1957 scheme, trustees instituted a small charge toward the cost of heating and lighting, producing during the 1960s and early 1970s an average sum of just under £200 a year. After the rebuilding of the Jane Sabina Collard Almshouses and the refurbishment of the Mary Squire Almshouses in 1975, however, total contributions from residents rose sharply to £2,620. At their meeting on 17 October 1974, the trustees set the contributions for the residents of the new Collard Almshouses at £3 a week for a single flat and £5 a week for a double flat. Charges for meals were set at £2.80 a week for each resident. Returning to the subject of contributions at the next meeting on 21 November, the trustees added 'a charge of 50p per flat to be contributed by the occupant for Heat and Lighting'.[23] As fuel and maintenance costs increased during the 1970s and 1980s, driven by the energy crisis and spiralling inflation, so did residents' contributions. By 1999, weekly maintenance contributions for Collard residents had risen to £36 for a single flat and £46 for a double flat, and weekly contributions toward heating and lighting to £10 for a single flat and £12 for a double. Before provision of midday meals was discontinued in 1998, the cost of meals had risen to £15 a week for each resident. Similar increases in maintenance contributions, reflecting the major refurbishment of the almshouses during the 1990s, were set for the residents of the Mary Squire Almshouses and the Sir George Monoux Almshouses, rising from £26 a month for each resident in 1991 to £143 a month for a single flat and £180 for a double flat in 1999. Altogether annual contributions from residents have risen from £180 in 1960 to £53,464 in 1999.[24]

The third fundamental change ordered by the 1957 scheme relates to the rebuilding and improvement of the existing almshouses and provision of further almshouses.[25] Armed with their new powers to spend income, and if necessary capital, on the repair and refurbishment of the almshouses, the trustees pressed ahead with the modernisation of the remaining almshouses in the east wing of the Sir George Monoux Almshouses. The plans of Darcy Braddell would have required total expenditure in the region of £36,000, and as a result the trustees sought advice from yet another architect, John E.M. Macgregor of Great Ormond Street, London. On 12 November 1956 Macgregor produced an initial report.[26] By using both the ground floor and the first floor of the east wing and by converting the Old Master's House, Macgregor's plan would provide two almshouses suitable for married couples with bedroom, kitchen and bathroom, and eight almshouses suitable for single people with bed-sitting rooms, kitchens, and shared sanitary facilities. The 19th-century rear extensions and outdoor w.c.s would be removed. Work began in 1960 and was completed in 1963 at a total cost of £11,718 8s. 4d. plus architect's and surveyor's fees of £1,133 6s. 3d.[27] An improvement grant from the Walthamstow Borough Council contributed £3,874 toward the cost; and by drawing £1,200 from the newly established Extraordinary Repair Fund and securing Charity Commission approval for another overdraft of £5,000 from Barclays Bank, the trustees were able to carry out the improvements entirely from current income.[28]

When the trustees had finished paying off their overdraft, they turned their attention to the modernisation of the Jane Sabina Collard Almshouses. Advising that the late Victorian almshouses could not conveniently be expanded or modernised, a surveyor's report by G. Ernest Clarke & Co. in June 1966 recommended the acquisition of the adjacent properties at 1 Maynard Road and 1 to 4 Beulah Path and the subsequent redevelopment of the site into a modern almshouse complex.[29] The trustees agreed, and over the next four years they acquired the necessary properties: 1 Maynard Road for £5,500 in 1966, 1 Beulah Path for £3,700 and 3 Beulah Path for £2,000 in 1967, 2 Beulah Path for £3,800 in 1969, and 4 Beulah Path for £6,000 in 1970.[30] Under the chairmanship of Alderman Walter Frank Savill, who served as Chairman of the Trustees from 1969 to 1976, the project quickly moved forward. In 1971, trustees approved plans by architect F.G. Southgate for a two-storey complex arranged around three sides of a courtyard and containing 12 single flats with bed-sitting room, bathroom and kitchen, and 12 double flats with separate bedroom, living room, kitchen and bathroom. In addition there would be a matron's flat, an office, a sick room, a main kitchen, a communal dining room, and a sun lounge.[31] Demolition work at the site began in December 1972 and was completed by Redbridge Demolition Co. Ltd. on 20 February 1973 at a cost of £2,700. On 7 March 1973, J. & J. Dean (Contracts) Limited submitted a tender of £211,592.54 for building the new almshouses. A Charity Commission Sealed Order dated 18 May 1973 approved expenditure of £219,200 for the new Collard Almshouses,

subject to a sinking fund being established
to recoup the cost over the next 60 years,
and four days later on 22 May the trustees
signed the building contract with
completion scheduled for 5 August 1974.[32]
Inclement weather, problems with the firm
supplying the prefabricated roof trusses,
and increased work to protect the foundations and boiler house from underground
water all delayed the completion date, but
on 13 December 1974 the new almshouses
were finished at a final cost of £224,479.92.
At a ceremony on 11 January 1975 the new
almshouses were officially declared open
by F.X. Houghton, grandson of one of Jane
Sabina Collard's orginal trustees, William
Houghton.[33]

Even as the contractors were clearing
the site and excavating the foundations for
the new Collard Almshouses on Maynard
Road, the trustees instructed G. Ernest
Clarke & Co. to survey the Mary Squire
Almshouses and prepare a conversion

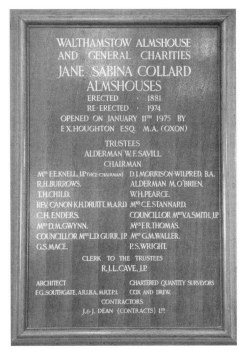

54   Plaque on the rebuilding of the Jane Sabina
Collard Almshouses in 1974.

scheme for renovation of the kitchens and provision of internal bathrooms and central
heating. Work began in March 1974 and was completed in March 1975. Externally the
almshouses could not be altered, since they were listed buildings, but all external
brickwork was repointed, a damp course was inserted, and doors and windows were
replaced. Internally, all wooden partitions and wooden floors, mostly damp and rotting,
were removed, and concrete flooring was laid. The rear extension was reconstructed
to include a small bathroom and toilet and a fully equipped kitchen. An efficient hot
water system was installed along with central heating in the form of night storage
heaters. Final costs of the improvements to the six almshouses amounted to £23,918.77,
including £318.36 for six new electric cookers. The London Borough of Waltham
Forest awarded Improvement Grants amounting to £5,986, leaving a net cost to the
trustees of £17,932.77. On 7 April 1975 the Charity Commission approved the final
expenditure and ordered the the trustees to make annual payments of £277.92 for 30
years into a sinking fund to recoup the expenditure, which had come primarily from
the sale of land on Boundary Road belonging to the Charity of Thomas Gamuel.[34]
Bearing in mind the increased value of the new Jane Sabina Collard Almshouses and
the renovated Mary Squire Almshouses, the Charity Commission on 16 April 1974
increased the annual payments to the Extraordinary Repair Fund to £1,350 and on
30 April 1975 increased the amount again to a yearly sum of £2,025.[35]

Improvements to the almshouses during the 1970s concluded with further works to the Sir George Monoux Almshouses. Following a report by the architect F.G. Southgate, the trustees on 23 September 1976 approved the modernisation of the kitchens in the 14 Monoux almshouses, including the installation of stainless steel sinks, new cookers, refrigerators and cupboards. A contract was signed on 21 July 1977 with J. Stichbury Limited of Harlow, Essex to carry out the work at a cost of £4,427.[36] Finally, in 1978 the trustees decided to convert the Monoux schoolroom into a committee room for the trustees and an office for the clerk. Since 1966 the first floor room had been used as a schoolroom for the St Mary's Church of England Infants School. In 1977, the trustees had explored the possibility of converting the large room into a flat for the almshouse nurse, but eventually they commissioned their architect T.L. Rampton to prepare plans for the conversion to a committee room. Rampton proposed an oak and glass partition to separate the office from the meeting room, the installation of pendant lighting, and the purchase of table and chairs for the board room and furniture for the office. Work began in the summer of 1979 and was completed in 1980 at a total cost of £10,775.26.[37]

During the final decade of the 20th century another round of improvements to the almshouses took place under the chairmanship of Mrs. Violet A. Smith. On 20 June 1991 the trustees appointed a Sub-Committee on Refurbishment to oversee the eventual improvement and modernisation of all the almshouse properties. Original plans for extending and modernising the bed-sitting rooms of the Mary Squire Almshouses were refused a Major Repair Grant from the Housing Corporation, and at the suggestion of The Almshouse Association alternative designs of almshouse architect Ernest J. Lowe were considered for converting the six bed-sitting rooms into four one-bedroom flats. In February 1995 CUBE Architects of Chingford were engaged to oversee the conversion, which provided four flats with separate bedrooms and living rooms, fully-fitted kitchens, and bathrooms equipped with low-level bath, shower with safety seat, safety rails, and non-slip floor surfaces. The work carried out by J.T. Luton at cost of £113,691.81 was completed in October 1995, but trustees had already turned their attention to the refurbishment of the Sir George Monoux Almshouses.

On 22 September 1995 CUBE Architects presented a feasibility study for a low-level rear extension of the Monoux Almshouses and the conversion of the two one-bedroom flats and 12 bed-sitting rooms into 12 one-bedroom flats plus a warden's flat, a warden's office, and a common room for the residents. The contract was awarded to Forest Gate Construction Limited on 29 October 1996, and the work was completed in August 1997 at a final cost of £556,293.18. On 18 October 1997 at a ceremony held in a marquee erected in the almshouse garden, Major General Anthony deC. L. Leask, Director of The Almshouse Association unveiled a plaque and officially declared the refurbished almshouses open.

In December 1997 the trustees commissioned a further feasibility study for similar conversion work of the bed-sitting rooms in the Jane Sabina Collard Almshouses. CUBE Architects proposed the creation of 12 flats for single pensioners and six flats for married

55 Vice-Chairman of the Trustees, Mrs. Janet Lewis, and Director of The Almshouse Association, Major General Anthony deC. L. Leask CB CBE, at the opening of the refurbished Sir George Monoux Almshouses.

56 *Above left.* Chairman of the Trustees Mrs. Violet Smith JP inspecting the kitchens of the refurbished Mary Squire's Almshouses.

57 *Above right.* Resident Warden Mrs. Irene Davies inspecting the progress of the refurbished Collard Court.

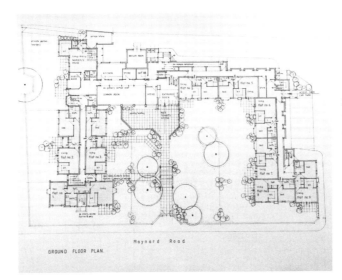

58-60 *Left.* Ground-floor plan of the refurbished Collard Court. *Below left.* The brass plaque in the lobby. *Below right.* The exterior of the refurbished Collard Court.

couples, each flat containing new fitted kitchens, lounge, separate bedroom, and bathrooms equipped with safety rails and level access showers. In addition to upgrading the flats for residents, the refurbishment included the installation of a lift, a new main entrance facing Maynard Road, a warden's office, a self-contained warden's apartment, a guest room, and a common room for residents. The contract was awarded to Collier Contracts Limited in July 1998, and work was completed by July 1999 at a cost of around £1.2 million. At the opening ceremony on 22 January 2000, almost twenty-five years to the day since the opening ceremony of the rebuilt Collard Almshouses on 11 January 1975, Director of The Almshouse Association, Major General Anthony deC. L. Leask CB CBE, praised the trustees of the Walthamstow Almshouse and General Charities for using their resources to provide up-to-date housing of the highest standard for the poor of Walthamstow.

Twelve

Financing the Future

ALTHOUGH THE 1957 CHARITY COMMISSION SCHEME significantly altered the charitable activity of the Walthamstow Almshouse and General Charities, even more significant have been the financial changes that have followed the establishment of the new scheme, changes that have provided the resources for the major almshouse refurbishments of the 20th century and changes that will continue to finance the future activity of the Walthamstow charities. Under their new title the trustees of the Walthamstow Almshouse and General Charities, first of all, continued to attract both additional bequests and the assets and administration of additional charities during the second half of the 20th century. The first direct bequest came in the year following the establishment of the new scheme. In 1935, Sir William Mallinson had founded the Charity of Sir William Mallinson in aid of the Connaught Hospital. Following the establishment of the National Health Service in 1948 and the subsequent state funding of the Connaught Hospital, the Charity Commission divided the endowments of the Mallinson Charity into four equal parts, establishing The Mallinson Fund in Aid of the William Mallinson Scholarship Trust, The Mallinson Fund in Aid of the Walthamstow Child Welfare Society, the Mallinson Fund in aid of the Connaught Hospital Amenities Fund, and The Mallinson Fund in aid of the Walthamstow Almshouse and General Charities. The assets before division consisted of £8,740 2s. 4d. invested in shares. The trustees of the Walthamstow Almshouse and General Charities were directed by the Charity Commission Scheme dated 18 July 1958 to apply the yearly income of their share 'for the general purposes of the Walthamstow Almshouse and General Charities except the charity of Sir Henry Maynard.'[1] A second bequest came in the Will dated 14 November 1963 of Mary Ann Caroline Richardson, a widow living at 174 Palmerston Road in Walthamstow, who left the residue of her estate to the Walthamstow Almshouse and General Charities. She died on 11 May 1967, and on 26 May 1970 the Trustees received a cheque from her executors for £7,413 7s. 8d. This sum was eventually deposited with the Official Custodian for Charities and invested for the purposes of the general maintenance of the charities.[2] A third bequest came from Miss Hilda Beatrice Slack, a resident of the Jane Sabina

Collard Almshouses from 11 January 1975 until her death on 10 December 1984. In her Will Miss Slack left to the Collard Almshouses the sum of £500 'for the purchase of a wooden six tiered structure for the display of potted plants together with a small lidded box for pots and tools'.[3] The most recent and the largest bequest came from Elizabeth M.A. Gillette, who by her Will dated 10 September 1976 left most of her estate to the Walthamstow Almshouse and General Charities 'for general income purposes'. Elizabeth Gillette died on 15 April 1990, and on 13 May 1991 the trustees received the sum of £43,733.64 from the sale of the premises at 15 Wellington Road.[4]

In addition to these bequests, the trustees of the Walthamstow Almshouse and General Charities also assumed control of the assets and administration of two additional charities: the Walthamstow Sick and Needy Fund in 1975 and the Chingford Almshouse Charities in 1980. Established by a Charity Commission scheme dated 11 March 1952, the Sick and Needy Fund had distributed food parcels at Christmas and from 1960 also at Easter. Owing to the difficulty in finding new trustees, the remaining trustees of the Sick and Needy Fund had voted on 12 March 1974 to close the Trust, but on 23 May 1974 the trustees of the Walthamstow Almshouse and General Charities agreed to accept the assets and administration of the Trust. The assets included £2,843.77 in shares and £145.71 in cash, yielding an annual income of approximately £100. By a scheme dated 15 January 1975 the Charity Commission created the Walthamstow Sick and Needy Fund and transferred its administration to the trustees of the Walthamstow Almshouse and General Charities with the remit 'to relieve in cases of need persons resident in the area of the former Borough of Walthamstow who are sick, convalescent, disabled, handicapped or infirm'.[5]

The most significant addition to the other trusts administered by the Walthamstow Almshouse and General Charities came on 16 June 1980, when the charity trustees accepted the assets and administration of the five charities known collectively as the Chingford Almshouse Charities and the management of their almshouses in Templeton Avenue in Chingford. In 1859, the same year that Jane Sabina Collard had established her almshouse charity in Walthamstow, four almshouses were built at The Green in Chingford at a total cost of £205 10s. 5d. raised by public subscription. A fifth house was added during the Jubilee of Queen Victoria in 1887. Over the next century other Chingford residents left legacies 'for repair and maintenance of the almshouse and for benefit of the poor occupants thereof', including £1,000 from Anne Ainslie in 1880, an additional £1,000 from her sister Elizabeth Ainslie in 1901, £100 from Mary Hartwell in 1922, and £100 from Edith Sarah Young in 1937. In her Will proved 5 July 1939, Nelly Ridgers left a house to be sold, requesting that the proceeds be applied to the almshouses at the trustees' discretion. The house was eventually sold in 1956 for £3,675 and the proceeds invested. The five almshouses and the endowments were administered by the rector and churchwardens of Chingford until 21 June 1957, when a Charity Commission scheme created the Chingford Almshouse Charities to be managed by seven trustees including the rector and churchwardens as ex-officio trustees,

61   The foundation stone of the enlarged Chingford Almshouses.

62   Victorian Almshouses on the Green in Chingford.

two representative trustees nominated by the Borough Council of Chingford and the Chingford Old People's Welfare Committee, and two co-optative trustees.[6]

At their first meeting on 20 September 1957, the trustees of The Chingford Almshouse Charities heard that two of the five existing almshouses were empty and, according to their architect, that 'the existing structures were not capable of modification or conversion so as to bring them into line with present day requirements.' In February 1958 the trustees resolved to purchase a new site on Templeton Avenue, offered for sale at £850 by the Chingford Borough Council, and to erect six new almshouses, each containing kitchen, bathroom and bed-sitting room. On 30 May the Chingford Nursing Association made a grant of £3,000 toward the erection of the new almshouses, and in September a public appeal was launched to raise a further £5,000. Posters and collecting boxes were exhibited by shopkeepers, and by February 1959 sufficient money had been raised for the trustees to sign a contract with P.G. Evans & Son for the construction of the new almshouses. The mayor of Chingford, as part of the celebrations marking the 21st anniversary of the granting of a charter of incorporation to the Borough of Chingford, officially declared the new almshouses open at a ceremony on 23 September 1959, almost one hundred years to the day after the old almshouses on the Green were originally opened on 22 July 1859.[7] A new Charity Commission scheme for the administration of the six new almshouses, dated 5 February 1960, authorised the trustees to sell the old almshouses on The Green for £200 and to apply the proceeds of sale toward the cost of erecting the new almshouses.[8]

Almost all of the resources of the Chingford Almshouse Charities had been used to meet the final building cost of £11,245.81, and during the 1960s and 1970s the trustees struggled to keep pace with inflation and spiralling fuel costs. The 1960 scheme

63 The Ridgers Almshouses erected in 1960 on Templeton Avenue.

had authorised the trustees to charge the almspeople weekly contributions of not more than 15s. toward the cost of fuel, and the Charity Commission authorised further increases in contributions to £3.25 a week in 1975 and £6 a week in 1979.[9] The parish of Chingford had four small coal charities, whose income had been used to heat the old almshouses: £400 given by John Popplewell in 1820 and his sisters Ann and Rebecca Popplewell in 1831, the Widows' Grass Charity that was distributed to poor widows at Christmas, £180 given by Harriet Waters in 1879, and £1,000 given by Mrs. Eliza King in 1916. In 1968 the Charity Commission allowed the income from these charities to be applied to electric heating, and in 1969 central heating was installed in the almshouses by the Eastern Electricity Board at a cost of £407 18s. 6d. In the face of sustained inflation, Chingford voluntary organisations held a May Fair in aid of the almshouses on 6 May 1972 and raised net proceeds of £2,112.31, which were invested for the maintenance and upkeep of the almshouses.[10]

In spite of all these efforts the Chingford Almshouse Charities continued to struggle against rising costs. Finally, at a meeting of the trustees on 25 May 1979, the imminent retirements of Miss Marjorie Block, who had served as a trustee and almshouse visitor since 1963; of John Carrington, the former borough treasurer who had served as honorary treasurer; and of A.S. Coldham, a solicitor who had served as clerk to the trustees, brought to a head the issue of the future of the Chingford Almshouse Charities. The trustees resolved 'to seek an amalgamation or a working arrangement with a larger Almshouse Charity which had available permanent Officers and Staff capable of giving the care and attention so necessary for the Almspeople and also of providing efficient administration.'[11] Exploratory meetings were arranged with the Walthamstow Almshouse and General Charities in June 1979, leading ultimately in 1980 to the transfer of assets totalling £28,066.24, including almshouses valued at the 1960 building cost of £11,245.81 but valued for insurance purposes at £147,000. A new Charity Commission Scheme ordered that the five charities comprising the Chingford Almshouse Charities 'shall be administered and managed' by the trustees of the Walthamstow Almshouse and General Charities.[12]

Even more significant than gaining the assets and administration of a new group of almshouses were the dramatic changes in the charity finances during the years following the 1957 Charity Commission scheme, changes both to charity income and charity assets.[13] First and foremost has been the increase in charity income during the last forty years of the 20th century. During the 1960s the annual income of the Walthamstow Almshouse and General Charities maintained a steady average of £7,649, but during the 1970s it began to rise sharply. Between 1970 and 1974 the average annual charity income more than tripled, rising to £23,698; and between 1975 and 1979 it tripled again, rising to £68,804. The rate of increase slowed during the 1980s, but by the end of the decade income had more than doubled to an annual average of £158,400. Spectacular gains during the 1990s, however, surpassed even these increases. Significant property sales, taking the charity income during 1992 and 1997 well above £1,000,000, pushed up the average annual income during the first half of the decade to £654,247 and during the second half of the decade to £915,635. Looked at another way, the annual charity income in 1960 was £5,972 compared to annual income in 1999 of £578,069—almost a hundredfold increase.

What caused this dramatic increase in charity income? The primary impetus for the rise in charity income since the 1957 Charity Commission scheme has been the sustained transfer of the capital assets of the charities from property to stocks and shares. The assets of the Walthamstow Almshouse and General Charities listed in the Schedule to the 1957 scheme showed a total annual income of £5,201 2s. with £2,023 5s. (39 per cent) arising from property and £3,177 17s. (61 per cent) arising from dividends and interest. A comparison of the sources of income in 1960 with sources of income in 1999, however, reveals a sharp decrease in the percentage of income arising from property and a corresponding increase in the percentage of income arising from dividends and interest. In 1960, the total income from these sources had risen to £5,754, comprising £3,900 (67.7 per cent) from dividends, £1,821 (31.7 per cent) from

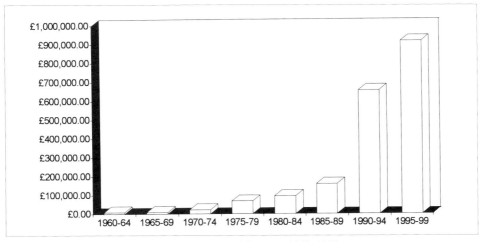

64   Average annual income, 1960-1999.

rents and rentcharges, and just £33 (0.6 per cent) from interest. In 1999, when the total income from these three sources had increased to £480,203, £334,740 (69.7 per cent) came from dividends, £125,072 (26 per cent) from interest, and just £20,391 (4.3 per cent) from property.

This transfer of capital assets from property to securities and the resulting shift in the sources of income began during the late 1960s for two primary reasons: the mandatory sale of most of the residential property belonging to the charities following the passage of the Leasehold Reform Act 1967 and the need to raise ready money for the rebuilding of the Jane Sabina Collard Almshouses. During the last quarter of the 19th century and the first quarter of the 20th century, much of the charity land had been let on long building leases to provide dwellinghouses for the rapidly expanding population of Walthamstow: property belonging to the Charity of Daniel Maclaurin on Havant Road for 99 years from 1904, property belonging to the Charity of Jane

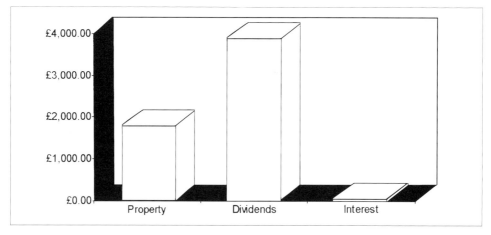

65 Charity income for 1960.

66 Charity income for 1999.

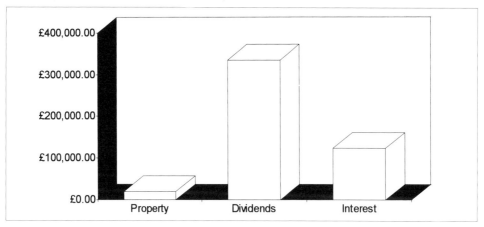

Sabina Collard on Albert Road and Hoe Street for 99 years from 1880 and on Maynard Road for 99 years from 1901, and property belonging to The Inhabitants Donation on Hempstead Road, Forest Road, and Fyfield Road for 99 years from 1881. In the neighbouring Borough of Leyton other property belonging to the Charity of Edmund Wise on Clarence Road, Toronto Road and Langthorne Road was let on similar building leases for 99 years from 1870.

Until the passage of the Leasehold Reform Act 1967, when a landlord let property on such long building leases and the builder then sold the leasehold of the newly constructed houses to tenants, the tenants paid the builder for their houses and paid ground rents to the landlord (usually being the original price of the lease to the builder divided by the number of houses built on the property). The leasehold of such houses belonged to the tenant, but the freehold of both the land and the houses remained the property of the landlord subject to the lease. Possession of both the land and the houses reverted to the landlord upon the expiration of the lease. Such building leases were often let for terms of 99 years, allowing the builder to sell the leasehold premises for prices equivalent to those of freehold premises. As the lease neared its end, however, the house rapidly depreciated in value to the leaseholder, but became a valuable and appreciating asset for the landlord to whom it would soon return.

Sympathetic to the plight of the diminishing assets of such leaseholders, the Labour government in 1967 passed the Leasehold Reform Act, giving qualified leaseholders the right to acquire the freehold of their house for the price of the site. If a tenant lived in a house under a long tenancy at a low ground rent, he could serve notice on the landlord, who would be obligated to convey the freehold of the house and premises or to grant a new extended tenancy. The price of the freehold depended on the capitalised value of the ground rents and the length of the unexpired term of the lease, but ignored completely the value of the house, which until the passage of the Act had been considered the property of the freeholder. The only way a landlord could refuse to convey the freehold was if he intended to live in the house as his principal residence or if he intended to redevelop the property. It was a good deal for tenants, but a poor deal for landlords and a poor deal for the trustees of the Walthamstow Almshouse and General Charities. Almost half of the charities' income arising from the property scheduled in the 1957 scheme came from these small ground rents on residential premises built on long building leases. Following the passage of the Leasehold Reform Act 1967, most of the occupiers of these properties gave notice that they wished to purchase the freehold, and the trustees had no option but to convey away the charity lands which they had held for centuries in trust for the poor of Walthamstow.[14]

About the same time that the Leasehold Reform Act 1967 began to take effect, the need to raise capital for the rebuilding of the Jane Sabina Collard Almshouses led to a further transfer of the capital assets of the charities from property to securities. By June 1966 the trustees had decided to demolish the Victorian almshouses on Maynard Road and redevelop the site. Over the next four years the trustees purchased the adjacent properties along Beulah Path and Maynard Road. Demolition work began in

February 1973, and construction of the new Collard Almshouses was completed in January 1975 at a final cost of £224,479.92. To raise the capital for land acquisition and construction, the trustees were authorised by the Charity Commission in 1969 to begin selling the residential properties on the south side of Maynard Road belonging to the Charity of Jane Sabina Collard and other property belonging to the Charity of Edmund Wise and the Charity of Thomas Gamuel, subject to the establishment of a sinking fund to recoup the expenditure over the next 60 years.[15]

The one silver lining in the statutory cloud of the Leasehold Reform Act, however, was that capital formerly tied up in property yielding low ground rents was released precisely at a time when property prices, share dividends and interest rates were all rapidly increasing. Houses on Maynard Road in Walthamstow, for example, and houses on Clarence Road, Langthorne Road, and Toronto Road in Leytonstone, each formerly yielding ground rents of £3 or less a year on long leases, were sold for prices ranging from £400 in 1969 to £9,000 in 1975.[16] As a result of these sales and the reinvestment of the proceeds pending payment of architects' certificates, total charity income continued to grow. Between 1965 and 1975, even after the costs of rebuilding the Collard Almshouses, the total charity income increased tenfold from £6,264 to £61,146; and income from interest and dividends during the same period increased sevenfold from £4,267 to £28,072. By 1980 investment income had more than doubled again to £61,213; and by 1990, when income from property rents amounted to only £43,708, income from investments had mushroomed to £509,546.

Dwarfing even the dramatic rise in charity income over the last four decades of the 20th century has been the rise in charity assets. This rise, beginning in 1969 and

67   Terrace houses on Maynard Road which were sold by the Charity Trustees in 1969.

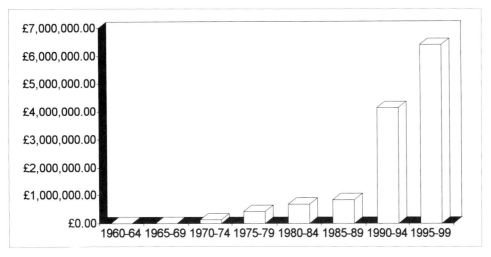

68   Average charity assets, 1960-1999.

keeping pace with the subsequent property sales, is partly due to the fact that the value of property that had been in the possession of the charities in some cases for several centuries was unknown and hence unrecorded in the annual balance sheet until it was sold. Even so the rise in charity assets, fuelled by a strong stock market and expanding economy, has been spectacular. During the 1960s the annual balance sheet showed average assets of £6,453. During the early '70s, led by property price increases and rising interest rates, average charity assets multiplied to £129,031 and during the second half of the decade to £423,779. By the end of the 1980s average charity assets had doubled again to £847,639. The quantum leap to £4,147,577 during the early 1990s resulted in part from the compulsory purchase by the Secretary of State for Transport of land belonging to the Charity of Thomas Colby for widening of the North Circular Road. During the second half of the decade other large property sales and sales of investments produced yet a further rise to an average of £6,370,326. Looked at another way, in 1960 the balance sheet showed assets of £6,876; in 1999 assets in the balance sheet had increased over a thousandfold to £7,505,714. When the unrealised value of share price increases was taken into consideration, the total charity assets during 1998 and 1999 were well over £10,000,000.

   With additional bequests approaching £100,000 and administration of new almshouses valued well over that figure, with a one-hundredfold increase in annual charity income from £5,972 to £578,069 and over a one-thousandfold increase in charity assets from £6,876 to £7,505,714, the Walthamstow Almshouse and General Charities has ended the final four decades of the 20th century in strong financial health; and the accumulated assets of five centuries of Walthamstow benefactors will continue to finance the future, as the Walthamstow charities enter a new millennium of caring for the poor.

Epilogue

Walthamstow in 2000

IN THE YEAR 1500 the churchwardens of St Mary's, Walthamstow administered one acre of land belonging to the Charity of the Rev. William Hyll. According to the earliest surviving churchwardens' accounts, that one acre of land yielded an annual rental income of £1. In the year 2000, after 500 years of accumulated charitable legacies from parish benefactors, the trustees of the Walthamstow Almshouse and General Charities administer land and investments worth well over £10,000,000. No one, not the churchwardens in 1500, not the Walthamstow Charity Governors in 1880 nor the trustees of the Walthamstow Parochial Charities in 1895, not even the new trustees of the Walthamstow Almshouse and General Charities in 1957 could have imagined the resources available to care for the poor at the beginning of the new millennium. Nor, as the Walthamstow Almshouse and General Charities enters the second 500 years of administering the Walthamstow charities, can even the present trustees imagine what the next 500 years will hold in store.

Nevertheless, one can look to the immediate future and to three challenges facing the current custodians of the Walthamstow charities. First, although census returns show that the population of Walthamstow peaked in 1931 at 132,972 and has since decreased steadily to 64,604 in the 1991 census, the population of the neighbouring Borough of Chingford has continued to rise throughout the 20th century from 4,373 in 1901 to 48,355 in 1951 to 70,462 in 1991. At the beginning of the new millennium, however, there are only six almshouses to meet the growing housing needs of the elderly poor in Chingford, six almshouses built in 1960 and now in need of renovation and refurbishment to bring them up to modern standards of care for the elderly. Although the trustees of the Walthamstow Almshouse and General Charities also function as trustees of the Chingford Almshouse Charities, current Charity Commission schemes keep the administration and assets of the two charities separate. The resources of the Walthamstow charities that have financed the programme of refurbishment of the Mary Squire's Almshouses, the Sir George Monoux Almshouses, and the Jane Sabina Collard Almshouses during the 1990s cannot currently be used for the provision of the almshouses in Chingford. A new Charity Commission scheme widening the beneficial area of the Walthamstow Almshouse and General Charities from the boundaries of the old Borough of Walthamstow to the boundaries of the new London Borough of Waltham Forest would allow the charity trustees to use their combined resources to meet the demands of housing and care for the elderly wherever they occur in the borough.

The changing nature of the population in the borough also offers its challenges. A second challenge facing the current custodians of the Walthamstow charities is the changing ethnic character of the London Borough of Waltham Forest. In the 1991 census 94 per cent of people between the ages of 65 and 74 were white, 98 per cent of the people between the ages of 75 and 84 were white, and 98 per cent of the people aged 85 and older were white. These are the pensioners currently catered for in the almshouses of the Walthamstow Almshouse and General Charities and the Chingford Almshouse Charities. If current trends continue, however, the elderly population of the London Borough of Waltham Forest will change dramatically over the next twenty to thirty years. Among those aged 55 to 64 in the 1991 census, blacks and ethnic minorities accounted for 17 per cent of the population. Among those aged 45 to 54 the percentage rises to 23 per cent; and among those aged 35 to 44 the percentage rises to 24 per cent. Among today's young people in the borough the percentage is even higher: black and ethnic minorities account for 31 per cent of those between 16 and 24, 41 per cent of those between 5 and 15, and 40 per cent of those 4 years old or younger. As the ethnic character of the pensioner population changes during the opening decades of the new millennium, so the Walthamstow Almshouse and General Charities will need to change and adapt its approach to include the increasing elderly black and Asian minorities of the borough.

A third challenge facing the current custodians of the Walthamstow charities is the increasing number of people living alone. Although the population of Walthamstow has declined by almost fifty percent since 1931, and although the overall population of the London Borough of Waltham Forest has declined steadily from 248,591 in 1961 to 212,033 in 1991, the number of people living alone, and in particular the number of elderly people living alone, has increased. In the 1991 census over one in seven people in the London Borough of Waltham Forest were pensioners, and over one in seven households contained pensioners living alone. As more people face the difficulties of growing old alone, there will be increased demand in the London Borough of Waltham Forest for the sheltered accommodation and subsidised housing offered by the Walthamstow Almshouse and General Charities for the elderly poor. With their current almshouse properties refurbished to modern standards, and armed with powers under their current Charity Commssion scheme for the provision of further almshouses, the Walthamstow Almshouse and General Charities is well placed at the beginning of the new millennium to meet the challenge of an increasingly elderly population not only by maintaining its ancient almshouses but also by providing new almshouses for a new millennium.

Appendix

Trustees of the
Walthamstow Charities

Trustees of the Walthamstow Parochial Charities appointed under the Charity Commission
Scheme of 4 October 1895

1895	John Anderson	St James Street Ward
	William Michael Beck	Wood Street Ward
	Ebenezer Clarke	Hoe Street Ward
	William Gower	Hoe Street Ward
	Eliot Howard	Co-optative
	The Rev. William H. Langhorne AKC	Ex-officio
	William McCall	Co-optative
	James Joseph McSheedy	St James Street Ward
	Rev. Frederic John Poole	Co-optative
	Walter W. Thompson	Northern Ward
	William Elliott Whittingham	Co-optative
1897	Charles James	High Street Ward
	W. Roberts	High Street Ward
1899	John Anderson	St James Street Ward
	William Michael Beck	Wood Street Ward
	William Gower	Hoe Street Ward
	James Joseph McSheedy	St James Street Ward
	Edward Archibald Simeon MD	Hoe Street Ward
	Walter W. Thompson	Northern Ward
1901	Caleb Day	Hoe Street Ward
1902	The Rev. Francis E. Murphy MA	Ex-officio
1903	T.R. Ballard	High Street Ward
	William Michael Beck	Wood Street Ward
	Edwin John Lucas	St James Street Ward
	Henry Osborne	Hoe Street Ward

	W. Roberts	High Street Ward
	Robert Thain	St James Street Ward
	Walter W. Thompson	Northern Ward
1904	Alvan Henry Edwards	High Street Ward
1905	Mr. Tomlin	Northern Ward
1906	George William Barker	Hoe Street Ward
1907	William Michael Beck	Wood Street Ward
	Henry Fergusson Inman Hallows	Wood Street Ward
	The Rev. Canon Herbert Dudley Lampen MA	Ex-officio
	James Sandeman	High Street Ward
	Thomas Scanlon	St James Street Ward
	Robert Thain	St James Street Ward
	Walter W. Thompson	Northern Ward
	Thomas Welham	Hoe Street Ward
	Charles Henry Wise MD	Co-optative
1908	Alvan Henry Edwards	High Street Ward
	John Higham	Co-optative

Trustees of the Walthamstow Parochial Charities appointed under the Charity Commission
Scheme of 5 June 1908

1909	John Cornelius Gillett	Co-optative
	Thomas How JP	Wood Street Ward
	George William Walkinshaw	Northern Ward
1910	George William Barker	Hoe Street Ward
1911	William Michael Beck	Wood Street Ward
	Charles Game	High Street Ward
	Thomas Scanlon	St James Street Ward
	Robert Thain	St James Street Ward
	Walter W. Thompson	Northern Ward
	Thomas Welham	Hoe Street Ward
1912	Alvan Henry Edwards	High Street Ward
	Frederick John Hitchman	Co-optative
	William Mallinson	Co-optative
1913	John Higham	Co-optative
	Thomas How JP	Wood Street Ward
	George William Walkinshaw	Northern Ward

Trustees of the Walthamstow Parochial Charities appointed under the Charity Commission
Scheme of 27 February 1914

1914	George William Barker	Hoe Street Ward
	Charles William Fisher	Higham Hill Ward
	John Cornelius Gillett	Co-optative
	Henry Pearce Martin JP	Wood Street Ward
	Walter Warrington	Hale End Ward
1915	William Michael Beck	Wood Street Ward
	Charles Game	High Street Ward
	Thomas Scanlon	St James Street Ward
	Robert Thain	St James Street Ward
	Walter W. Thompson	Higham Hill Ward
	Thomas Welham	Hoe Street Ward
1916	Alvan Henry Edwards	High Street Ward
	Edwin Reynolds	Higham Hill Ward
	E. Samuels	Hoe Street Ward
1917	Adolphus Attwell JP	Hoe Street Ward
	George William Walkinshaw	Hale End Ward
	Charles James Wilkes	Co-optative
1918	John Higham	Co-optative
	Henry Pearce Martin JP	Wood Street Ward
	William Tyler JP	Co-optative
	Walter Warrington	Hale End Ward
1919	William Michael Beck	Wood Street Ward
	Charles Game	High Street Ward
	Miss K.V. Jennings	Co-optative
	Thomas Scanlon	St James Street Ward
	Robert Thain	St James Street Ward
	Walter W. Thompson	Higham Hill Ward
	Thomas Welham	Hoe Street Ward
1920	A.E. Beckwith	High Street Ward
	Charles E. Buck	Higham Hill Ward
	Harry William Dongray	Wood Street Ward
1921	Adophus Attwell JP	Hoe Street Ward
	Bertram Cole	Hale End Ward
	Alvan Henry Edwards	Co-optative
	Captain Alfred Eve JP	Co-optative

	Percy Friedburg	High Street Ward
	Walter Warrington	Hale End Ward
1922	Henry Pearce Martin JP	Wood Street Ward
1923	Harry F. Norrish	St James Street Ward
	Robert Thain	St James Street Ward
	William Tyler JP	Co-optative
	W.E. Weedon	Higham Hill Ward
	Thomas Welham	Hoe Street Ward
1924	George F. Bosworth	Co-optative
	Charles E. Buck	Higham Hill Ward
	Harry William Dongray	Wood Street Ward
	W. Winningale	High Street Ward
1925	Adolphus Attwell JP	Hoe Street Ward
	Frank William Bailey	Hale End Ward
	E. Hyde Stokes	Hale End Ward
1926	George Bell	Hoe Street Ward
	E. Churcher	Hale End Ward
	Alvan Henry Edwards	Co-optative
	Percy Friedburg	High Street Ward
	W.J. McGuffie JP	Co-optative
	J.C. Hammond	Co-optative
	Henry Pearce Martin JP	Wood Street Ward
1927	G. Gibbons JP	St James Street Ward
	Harry F. Norrish	St James Street Ward
	The Rev. Canon George Douglas Oakley MA	Ex-officio
	Robert Thain	Higham Hill Ward
	Thomas Welham	Hoe Street Ward
1928	Charles E. Buck	Higham Hill Ward
	Walter Gillett	Wood Street Ward
	F.W. Harcourt	Hale End Ward
	W. Lawrence	High Street Ward
1929	Frank William Bailey	Hale End Ward
	George F. Bosworth	Co-optative
	Percy Friedburg	High Street Ward
1930	George Bell	Hoe Street Ward
	Captain Alfred Eve JP	Hoe Street Ward

	Beryl Anne Henderson	Wood Street Ward
	Henry Pearce Martin	Co-optative
1931	Alvan Henry Edwards	Co-optative
	G. Gibbons JP	St James Street Ward
	J.C. Hammond	Co-optative
	Harry F. Norrish	St James Street Ward
	Robert Thain	Higham Hill Ward
1932	Bertram Cole	Hale End Ward
	W. Lawrence	High Street Ward
	R.E. Smith	Wood Street Ward
1933	H.G. Bottomley	High Street Ward
	H.C. Dowell	Hale End Ward
	J. Mansfield	Higham Hill Ward
1934	George Bell	Hoe Street Ward
	George F. Bosworth	Co-optative
	Captain Alfred Eve JP	Hoe Street Ward
	Nellie McCarthy	Wood Street Ward
1935	Percy Friedburg	Co-optative
	G. Gibbons JP	St James Street Ward
	J.H. Hammond	High Street Ward
	Henry Pearce Martin	Hoe Street Ward
	Harry F. Norrish	St James Street Ward
1936	Percy Astins	Co-optative
	Thomas William Bacon	High Street Ward
	L. Priscilla Bailey	Hale End Ward
	J.E. Foster	Higham Hill Ward
	Walter Gillett	Hoe Street Ward
	J. Mansfield	Higham Hill Ward
	R.E. Smith	Wood Street Ward
1937	H.C. Dowell	Hale End Ward
	J.C. Hammond	Co-optative
1938	Nellie McCarthy	Wood Street Ward
1939	George F. Bosworth	Co-optative
	William George Frewin	High Street Ward
	G. Gibbons JP	St James Street Ward
	Albert Ernest Manning	St James Street Ward
	Henry Pearce Martin	Hoe Street Ward

1940	Thomas William Bacon	High Street Ward
	L. Priscilla Bailey	Hale End Ward
	Walter Gillett	Hoe Street Ward
	J. Mansfield	Higham Hill Ward
	William David Middleton	Higham Hill Ward
	R.E. Smith	Wood Street Ward
1941	Sarah Candy	Co-optative
	Percy Friedburg	Co-optative
	E.M. Richards	St James Street Ward
1942	Albert Crozier	Co-optative
	William Brown Fitt OBE	Co-optative
	Nellie McCarthy	Wood Street Ward
	A.L. Meadows	Hoe Street Ward
	P.G. Roberts	Hale End Ward
1943	Albert Ernest Manning	St James Street Ward
	William David Middleton	Higham Hill Ward
	Clara Emily Stannard	High Street Ward
1944	Thomas William Bacon	High Street Ward
	L. Priscilla Bailey	Hale End Ward
	Dorothy Florence Mabel Dyde	Higham Hill Ward
	William George Frewin	Co-optative
	Walter Gillett	Hoe Street Ward
	Walter Frank Savill	St James Street Ward
	Arthur Skinner	Co-optative
	Miss D. Wrigley	Wood Street Ward
1945	Frederick William Gentle	Hoe Street Ward
1946	Sarah Candy	Co-optative
	Albert Ernest Manning	St James Street Ward
	Nellie McCarthy	Wood Street Ward
	William David Middleton	Higham Hill Ward
	E.R. Spragg	Hale End Ward
	Clara Emily Stannard	High Street Ward
1947	Thomas William Bacon	High Street Ward
	Gertrude Bartlett	Hale End Ward
	Olive Berriff	Wood Street Ward
	Cyril William Victor Clayden	Hoe Street Ward
	Dorothy Florence Mabel Dyde	Higham Hill Ward
	William Brown Fitt OBE	Co-optative
	Walter Frank Savill	St James Street Ward

1948	Walter Gillett	Hoe Street Ward

1949	William George Frewin	Co-optative
	George Stanley Mace	Hale End Ward
	William David Middleton	Higham Hill Ward
	Arthur Skinner	Co-optative

1950	Albert Ernest Manning	St James Street Ward
	Montagu Sharland	Higham Hill Ward
	Clara Emily Stannard	High Street Ward

1951	Thomas William Bacon	Co-optative
	Margaret Joan Burton	Hoe Street Ward
	Constance Florence Davies	Hale End Ward
	The Rev. Canon Kenneth Harwood Druitt MA	Ex-officio
	Dorothy Florence Mabel Dyde	Higham Hill Ward
	Arthur Edward Harris	Wood Street Ward
	Walter Frank Savill	St James Street Ward
	Peter Frederick Webster	High Street Ward

1952	William Brown Fitt OBE	Co-optative
	Walter Gillett	Hoe Street Ward
	John Alexander Green	High Street Ward
	Doreen Stone	Wood Street Ward

| 1953 | George Stanley Mace | Hale End Ward |

1954	Edward John Collins	Wood Street Ward
	Emma Marie Christine Frewin	Co-optative
	Albert Ernest Manning	St James Street Ward
	Montagu Sharland	Higham Hill Ward
	Arthur Skinner	Co-optative
	Clara Emily Stannard	High Street Ward

1955	Joan Common	Hoe Street Ward
	Constance Florence Davies	Hale End Ward
	Dorothy Florence Mabel Dyde	Higham Hill Ward
	Charles Herbert Enders	Co-optative
	Nellie McCarthy	Wood Street Ward
	Walter Frank Savill	St James Street Ward

1956	Thomas William Bacon	Co-optative
	Terence Herbert Child	Hoe Street Ward
	Edmond Albert Thomason	High Street Ward

Trustees of the Walthamstow Almshouse and General Charities appointed under the
Charity Commission Scheme of 22 March 1957

1957	William Brown Fitt OBE	Co-optative
	George Stanley Mace	Hale End Ward
	S.E. White	St James Street Ward
1958	Wilfred Atkinson	Higham Hill Ward
	Charles James Crosbie	Wood Street Ward
	William David Middleton	Higham Hill Ward
	Clara Emily Stannard	High Street Ward
1959	Joan Common	Hoe Street Ward
	Constance Florence Davies	Hale End Ward
	Dorothy Florence Mabel Dyde	Higham Hill Ward
	Emma Marie Christine Frewin	Co-optative
	Walter Frank Savill	St James Street Ward
1960	Nellie Bingham	Wood Street Ward
	Terence Herbert Child	Hoe Street Ward
	Charles Herbert Enders	Co-optative
	Nellie McCarthy	Wood Street Ward
	Edmond Albert Thomason	High Street Ward
1961	Elsie Lilian Baldwin	Co-optative
	Gwendolen Florence Cowell	Hale End Ward
	George Stanley Mace	Hale End Ward
	Violet Alice Smith JP	Higham Hill Ward
	Hilda Jennie Swanton	St James Street Ward
1962	Thomas William Bacon	Co-optative
1963	Joan Common	Hoe Street Ward
	Doris Mafalda Gwynn	High Street Ward
	Wilfred Harry Pearce	Higham Hill Ward
	Walter Frank Savill	St James Street Ward
	Clara Emily Stannard	High Street Ward
1964	Terence Herbert Child	Hoe Street Ward
	Winifred Edith Irene Fox	Wood Street Ward
	Annette Pearson	Wood Street Ward
1965	Nellie Bingham	Co-optative
	Charles Herbert Enders	Co-optative
	George Stanley Mace	Hale End Ward

	Francis Augustine John O'Shea	Hale End Ward
	Violet Alice Smith JP	Higham Hill Ward
	Hilda Jennie Swanton	St James Street Ward
1966	Elsie Lilian Baldwin	Co-optative
	Clara Emily Stannard	High Street Ward
	Sylvia Weinstein	Co-optative
1967	Joan Common	Hoe Street Ward
	G.A. King	Hale End Ward
	A.M. O'Reilly JP	Wood Street Ward
	Wilfred Harry Pearce	Higham Hill Ward
	Walter Frank Savill	St James Street Ward
	Christopher J.W. Walker	High Street Ward
1968	Roy Henry Burrows	Co-optative
	Terence Herbert Child	Hoe Street Ward
	Doris Mafalda Gwynn	Co-optative
	Florence Elizabeth Knell JP	Hale End Ward
	George Richard Winters	Wood Streeet Ward
1969	Norman Arthur Lyons	Higham Hill Ward
	George Stanley Mace	Hale End Ward
	William Charles Warren	St James Street Ward
1970	Charles Herbert Enders	Co-optative
1971	Lilian Dorothy Gurr JP	Hoe Street Ward
	Lionel Ernest Gwynn	Co-optative
	David John Morrison-Wilpred BA	Wood Street Ward
	Wilfred Harry Pearce	Higham Hill Ward
	Walter Frank Savill	St James Street Ward
	Clara Emily Stannard	High Street Ward
	Christopher J.W. Walker	High Street Ward
1972	Daniel Thomas John Allen	Higham Hill Ward
	Florence Elizabeth Knell JP	Hale End Ward
	Martin O'Brien	Hoe Street Ward
	David Robert Staff	High Street Ward
	Grace May Waller JP	Wood Street Ward
1973	Terence Herbert Child	Co-optative
	Doris Mafalda Gwynn	Co-optative
	George Stanley Mace	Hale End Ward
1974	Roy Henry Burrows	Higham Hill Ward
	Violet Alice Smith JP	Co-optative

	Flora Rita Thomas	St James Street Ward
	Philip Sidney Wright	High Street Ward
1975	Lilian Dorothy Gurr JP	Hoe Street Ward
	Hazel Mary Husband	High Street Ward
	Betty Millard	St James Street Ward
	Winifred Martha Palethorpe JP	High Street Ward
	Wilfred Harry Pearce	Higham Hill Ward
	Brenda W. Sapsford	Wood Street Ward
	Walter Frank Savill	St James Street Ward
1976	John Philip Griggs	Co-optative
	Florence Elizabeth Knell JP	Hale End Ward
	Martin O'Brien	Hoe Street Ward
	Grace May Waller JP	Wood Street Ward
1977	Richard A. Baldwin	High Street Ward
	George Stanley Mace	Hale End Ward
	Hilda Jennie Swanton	St James Street Ward
1978	William George Anstey	Wood Street Ward
	Roy Henry Burrows	Higham Hill Ward
	Terence Herbert Child	Co-optative
	Doris Mafalda Gwynn	Co-optative
1979	Joan M. Christopher	Higham Hill Ward
	Lilian Dorothy Gurr JP	Hoe Street Ward
	Janet Lewis	Hale End Ward
	Betty Millard	St James Street Ward
	Winifred Martha Palethorpe JP	High Street Ward
	Brenda W. Sapsford	Wood Street Ward
	Violet Alice Smith JP	Co-optative
1980	Derrick Ernest Hainsworth	High Street Ward
	Caroline Hammond	Hoe Street Ward
1981	John Philip Griggs	Co-optative
	Robin A. Louis Henderson	Hoe Street Ward
	Florence Elizabeth Knell JP	Hale End Ward
1982	Eleanor Bartram	Hoe Street Ward
	Roy Henry Burrows	Higham Hill Ward
	Hilda Jennie Swanton	St James Street Ward
1983	Terence Herbert Child	Co-optative
	Joan M. Christopher	Higham Hill Ward
	Reginald B. Lewis FOB	Wood Street Ward
	D. Peacock	Wood Street Ward

1984	Christopher Foxton	Co-optative
	Doris Mafala Gwynn	Co-optative
	Derrick Ernest Hainsworth	High Street Ward
	Janet Lewis	Hale End Ward
	Betty Millard	St James Street Ward
	Violet Alice Smith JP	Co-optative
	The Rev. Peter J. Trendall	Ex-officio
1985	Robin A. Louis Henderson	Hoe Street Ward
	Florence Elizabeth Knell JP	Hale End Ward
	Edith Poulsen	High Street Ward
1986	Eleanor Bartram	Hoe Street Ward
	Roy Henry Burrows	Higham Hill Ward
	John Philip Griggs	Co-optative
	Garner R. Smith	Co-optative
	Hilda Jennie Swanton	St James Street Ward
	M.A. Wasserman	Higham Hill Ward
1987	Barbara Payling	Wood Street Ward
1988	William George Anstey	Wood Street Ward
	Derrick Ernest Hainsworth	High Street Ward
	Janet Lewis	Hale End Ward
	Reginald B. Lewis FOB	Co-optative
	Betty Millard	St James Street Ward
	Margaret Willett	Wood Street Ward
1989	Florence Elizabeth Knell JP	Hale End Ward
	Violet Alice Smith JP	Co-optative
1990	Robin A. Louis Henderson	Hoe Street Ward
	Frederick V. Lake	Wood Street Ward
	Martin O'Brien	Hoe Street Ward
	Edith Poulsen	High Street Ward
	Hilda Jennie Swanton	St James Street Ward
1991	Roy Henry Burrows	Higham Hill Ward
	George F. Coomber	Higham Hill Ward
	John Philip Griggs	Co-optative
	Garner R. Smith	Co-optative
1992	William George Anstey	Wood Street Ward
	Derrick Ernest Hainsworth	High Street Ward
	Janet Lewis	Hale End Ward
	Betty Millard	St James Street Ward

1993	Florence Elizabeth Knell JP	Hale End Ward
	Reginald B. Lewis FOB	Co-optative
1994	Barrie M.B. Bates	Co-optative
	The Rev. Paul Butler	Ex-officio
	Janet Dawe	Wood Street Ward
	Robin A. Louis Henderson	Hoe Street Ward
	Edith Poulsen	High Street Ward
	Norman Scotney	Wood Street Ward
	Violet Alice Smith JP	Co-optative
	Hilda Jennie Swanton	St James Street Ward
	Anita Tarshis	Hoe Street Ward
1995	Roy Henry Burrows	Higham Hill Ward
	George F. Coomber	Higham Hill Ward
1996	Wenda Belam	Higham Hill Ward
	Derrick Ernest Hainsworth	High Street Ward
	Tahir Kamal	St James Street Ward
	Frederick V. Lake	Wood Street Ward
	Janet Lewis	Hale End Ward
	Garner R. Smith	Co-optative
1997	Florence Elizabeth Knell JP	Hale End Ward
1998	George Arkless BA	Co-optative
	Janet Dawe	Wood Street Ward
	Betty Millard	St James Street Ward
	Edith Poulsen	High Street Ward
1999	Robin A. Louis Henderson	Hoe Street Ward
	Jean Croxton	Hoe Street Ward
	Phyllida Culpin	Wood Street Ward
	Hilda Jennie Swanton	St James Street Ward
	Barrie M.B. Bates	Co-optative
2000	Violet Alice Smith JP	Co-optative
	Janet Lewis	Hale End Ward

Notes

Introduction: Walthamstow in 1500

1. W.R. Powell, ed., *A History of Essex*, The Victoria County History of the Counties of England (Oxford University Press, 1973), VI:241.
2. H. Arthur Doubleday and William Page, eds., *The Victoria History of the Counties of England: Essex* (Westminster: Archibald Constable and Company Limited, 1903), I:537, 555-6.
3. W.R. Powell, ed., *A History of Essex*, VI:253-63.
4. William Page and J. Horace Round, eds., *The Victoria History of the County of Essex* (London: Archibald Constable and Company Limited, 1907), II:115-22, 166-72, 186-8.
5. Waltham Forest Archives: W47.1 Z1 'Some Particulars relating to the Parish of Walthamstow in the County of Essex. Extracted from Authentic Records in the Possession of a late Churchwarden, 1789', p. 87.
6. Waltham Forest Archives: W47.1/1, Vestry Minute Book, pp. 53-9.

Chapter One: George Monoux: Gentleman and Benefactor

1. S.T. Bindoff, *The History of Parliament: The House of Commons 1509-1588*, 3 vols. (London: Secker and Warburg, 1982), 2:611-13. *See also* George F. Bosworth, *George Monoux: The Story of a Walthamstow Worthy* (Walthamstow Antiquarian Society Official Publication No. 3, 1916), *passim*.
2. Steve Rappaport, *Worlds within Worlds: Structures of Life in 16th-century London* (Cambridge University Press, 1989), pp.195-201.
3. *Ibid.*, p.197.
4. *Ibid.*, p.199.
5. William Kitchener Jordan, *The Charities of London 1480-1660* (London: George Allen & Unwin Ltd., 1960), p.21.
6. *Ibid.*, p.48.
7. *Ibid.*, pp.64-5.
8. *Ibid.*, p.65.
9. *Ibid.*, pp.310-1, 426.
10. Although Monoux was granted a coat of arms in 1514 and after his death was frequently styled Sir George by the residents of Walthamstow, he was never knighted.
11. George F. Bosworth, *A History of Walthamstow Charities 1487-1920* (Walthamstow Antiquarian Society Official Publication No. 8, 1920), p.9.
12. British Library, Additional MS 18783, ff.5r-5v. Monoux's memorandum regarding the grant of the almshouse land is confirmed by an Agreement dated 14 January 1528 and entered in the Register of Bishop Tunstall, Bishop of London, f.151, a copy of which

appears in Waltham Forest Archives, MS W47.1 Z1, pp.79-81, entitled 'Some Particulars relating to the Parish of Walthamstow in the County of Essex Extracted from Authentic Records in the Possession of a late Churchwarden, 1789'.

13.   Waltham Forest Archives, DA400 A2/14/2, Inquisition, 4 August 1635, as quoted by George Bosworth and Constance Demain-Saunders, *Original Documents relating to the Monoux Family* (Walthamstow Antiquarian Society Official Publication No. 19, 1928), p.15; see also Waltham Forest Archives, W83.1 R2, 'Particulars of the Evidence concerning ye house yard & close adjoyning to ye Almshouses as they were deliver'd at the Inquisition taken at Stratford 4 Aug. 11 Car.'.

14.   Modernised from Monoux's original rules in the British Library, Additional MS 18783, Leiger Book of Estates of George Monoux 1508-1553, f.6r.

15.   Will of George Monoux, as quoted by Sir George S. Fry, *Abstracts of Wills relating to Walthamstow, Co. Essex (1335-1559)*, Old Monograph Series, No. 9 (Walthamstow Antiquarian Society, 1921), pp.21-6.

16.   As quoted by Bosworth, *A History of Walthamstow Charities*, p.55.

17.   Waltham Forest Archives, DA400 A2/14/2, as quoted by Bosworth and Demain-Saunders, *Original Documents relating to the Monoux Family*, pp.7-16.

18.   Waltham Forest Archives: W47.1 Z1. 'Some Particulars relating to the Parish of Walthamstow', p.82.

19.   *Ibid.*, pp.49-57.

20.   *Ibid.*, pp.58-73; Waltham Forest Archives: DA400 A2/14/3, Inquisition, 20 March 1658.

21.   Waltham Forest Archives: DA400 E2/13/1 Memorandum; W 47.1/1, Vestry Minute Book, p.114; W 47.1/2, Vestry Minute Book, p.64.

Chapter Two: The Parish Poor Law System

 1.   As quoted by Sidney and Beatrice Webb, *English Poor Law History*, 3 vols. (Frank Cass and Co. Ltd., 1963), I:46 .

 2.   F.R. Salter, ed., *Some Early Tracts on Poor Relief* (1926), pp.80-96.

 3.   Webb, *English Poor Law History*, I:46.

 4.   *The Statutes at Large* (London, 1786), II: 671-2.

 5.   *Ibid.*, II:671, 685-8.

 6.   The British Library, Harley MS 7020, f.267.

 7.   *The Statutes at Large* (London, 1786), III: 223-6.

 8.   Public Record Office, SP16, vol. 183, No. 60.

 9.   Public Record Office, SP16, vol. 329, No. 48.

10.   Waltham Forest Archives: W47.1/1, Vestry Minute Book, p.52.

11.   *Ibid.*, p.137.

12.   *Ibid.*, p.47.

13.   *Ibid.*, pp.105-10. Abbreviations in this and all subsequent quotations have been silently expanded.

14.   *Ibid.*, p.131.

15.   *Ibid.*, pp.150-1.

16.   *Ibid.*, p.67.

17.   *Ibid.*, p.129.

18. Waltham Forest Archives: W 47.1/2, Vestry Minute Book, p.30.

19. Waltham Forest Archives: W 47.1/1, p.120.

20. *Ibid.*, pp.17-18.

21. *Ibid.*, p.257.

22. *Ibid.*, p.110.

23. *Ibid.*, p.150.

24. *Ibid.*, p.134.

25. Waltham Forest Archives: W 47.1/2, pp.30-1.

Chapter Three: The 17th-Century Charities

1. Waltham Forest Archives, DA400 Z1/4: Report of the Commissioners for Inquiring Concerning Charities, 10 July 1833, p.157; Bosworth, *A History of Walthamstow Charities*, pp.13-14.

2. Waltham Forest Archives, W47.1 Z1: 'Some Particulars relating to the Parish of Walthamstow', pp.88-9; *see also* Commissioners Report, p.151; Bosworth, *A History of Walthamstow Charities*, pp.16-17.

3. 'Some Particulars', pp.90-2, 95-7; Commissioners Report, pp.151-2; Bosworth, *A History of Walthamstow Charities*, pp.17-19.

4. Waltham Forest Archives, W47.1/1, pp.54, 97, 101-2, 170-2, 177-80; 'Some Particulars', pp.101, 104; Commissioners Report, pp.152-3; Bosworth, *A History of Walthamstow Charities*, pp.30-2; W 47.1/2, p.15.

5. Commissioners Report, pp.160-1; Bosworth, *A History of Walthamstow Charities*, pp.14-16.

6. Waltham Forest Archives, DA400 E2/2A/1, Abstract of Conveyance.

7. Waltham Forest Archives, DA400 E2/10A/1, Abstract of Indenture of Feoffment; *see also* Commissioners Report, pp.158-60; Bosworth, *A History of Walthamstow Charities*, pp.19-21.

8. Waltham Forest Archives, DA400 E2/5/1, Will of Edward Corbett; 'Some Particulars', pp.82, 97-8; Commissioners Report, pp.161-2; Bosworth, *A History of Walthamstow Charities*, pp.21-2.

9. Waltham Forest Archives: DA400 A2/13/1, Will of Henry Maynard.

10. Waltham Forest Archives: DA400 E2/12A/1, Release, 4 November 1690, and DA400 E2/12A/2, Conveyance, 1 March 1691.

11. 'Some Particulars', pp.106-11; DA400 A2/13/2, Inquisition.

12. Waltham Forest Archives: DA400 A2/13/3, Case for Exceptant.

13. Waltham Forest Archives: DA400 A2/13/4, Case for Respondents.

14. Waltham Forest Archives: DA400 A2/13/5, Court Proceedings.

15. Waltham Forest Archives: DA400 A2/13/6, Master's Report, 5 April 1714; A2/13/7, Court Order, 13 August 1714; A2/13/8, Master's Report, 23 October 1717; and A2/13/9, Court Order, 29 November 1720.

16. Waltham Forest Archives: W47.1/1, pp.53-9, 88.

Chapter Four: Setting the Poor to Work

1. 43 Elizabeth, c.2, in *The Statutes at Large* (London, 1786), II: 685-8.

2.   Waltham Forest Archives: W47.1/1, pp.75-6.

3.   *Ibid.*, p.82.

4.   9 George I. c.7, in *The Statutes at Large*, V: 307-9.

5.   *An Account of Several Work-Houses for Employing and Maintaining the Poor* (London, 1725), pp.51-62.

6.   Waltham Forest Archives: W47.1/1, p.144.

7.   *Ibid.*, p.145.

8.   *Ibid.*, p.146.

9.   *Ibid.*, pp.147-8.

10. *Ibid.*, pp.137, 152.

11. *Ibid.*, p.183.

12. *Ibid.*, p.190.

13. *Ibid.*, pp.213-14.

14. As quoted in Roy Porter, *English Society in the Eighteenth Century* (London: Allen Lane, 1982), p.147.

15. Waltham Forest Archives: W34.41 A1, Workhouse Account Book.

16. Porter, *English Society in the Eighteenth Century*, pp.147-8.

17. Waltham Forest Archives: W47.1/2, p.83.

18. Waltham Forest Archives: W47.1/1, p.346.

19. *Ibid.*, pp.352-4.

20. Waltham Forest Archives: W47.1/4, Vestry Minute Book, pp.155-6.

21. *Ibid.*, pp.176-7.

22. *Ibid.*, p.352.

23. Waltham Forest Archives: W34.41 M3, Workhouse Management Committee Minute Book.

24. Waltham Forest Archives: W47.1/1, pp.146, 190; W47.1/2, p.60.

25. Waltham Forest Archives: W47.1/2, p.302.

26. *Ibid.*, p.319.

27. *Ibid.*, p.354.

28. Waltham Forest Archives: W47.1/3, Vestry Minute Book, p.31.

29. *Ibid.*, pp.164, 219, 288.

30. *Ibid.*, pp.315, 338, 360.

31. Waltham Forest Archives: W47.1/4, pp.41, 60.

32. *Ibid.* p.160.

33. Waltham Forest Archives: W34.41 M2, Workhouse Management Committee Minute Book.

34. Waltham Forest Archives: W47.1/2, p.156.

35. Waltham Forest Archives: W47.1/3, p.317.

36. Waltham Forest Archives: W34.41 M4, Workhouse Management Committee Minute Book.

37. Porter, *English Society in the Eighteenth Century*, p.145.

38. 22 George III, c. 83, in *The Statutes at Large*, IX: 268-83.

Chapter Five: Life in the Workhouse

1.   *The Village: A Poem in Two Books By The Rev. George Crabbe* (London, MDCCLXXXIII), pp.15-17.

2.   Waltham Forest Archives: W47.1/1, p.270.

3.   Waltham Forest Archives: W47.1/2, pp.24, 34.

4.   *Ibid.*, p.158.

5.   Waltham Forest Archives: W47.1/4, p.46.

6.   *Ibid.*, p.142.

7.   Waltham Forest Archives: W47.1/2, p.159.

8.   *Ibid.*, pp.159-308.

9.   Waltham Forest Archives: W34.41 M4, Workhouse Management Committee Minute Book.

10. Waltham Forest Archives: W47.1/1, pp.58, 131.

11. *Ibid.*, p.258.

12. Waltham Forest Archives: W47.1/2, pp. 33, 40; W47.1/3, p.45.

13. Waltham Forest Archives: W47.1/4, p.70.

14. Waltham Forest Archives: W47.1/5, Vestry Minute Book, pp.166, 176.

15. *Ibid.*, p.278.

16. Waltham Forest Archives: W47.1/4, pp.168, 171.

17. Waltham Forest Archives: W47.1/5, pp.314, 319.

18. Waltham Forest Archives: W34.41 M3, Workhouse Management Committee Minute Book.

19. Waltham Forest Archives: W47.1/2, p.355.

20. Waltham Forest Archives: W47.1/4, pp.174-6.

21. *Ibid.*, pp.45-6.

22. *Ibid.*, pp.171-2.

23. *Ibid.*, p.171.

24. Waltham Forest Archives: W47.1/2, p.15.

25. *Ibid.*, p.60.

26. Waltham Forest Archives: W47.1/4, p.50.

27. *Ibid.*, pp.376, 399, 441, 457, 478, 496, 510, 533, and W47.1/5, *passim*.

28. Waltham Forest Archives: W47.1/4, p.71.

29. *Ibid.*, pp.173-4.

30. *Ibid.*, pp.169-70.

31. *Ibid.*, pp.181-2.

32. *Ibid.*, p.187.

33. Waltham Forest Archives: W47.1/5, p.208; Waltham Forest Archives: W34.41 M3, Workhouse Management Committee Minute Book.

Chapter Six: The 18th-Century Charities

1.   Waltham Forest Archives: W47.1/1, p.140.

2.   *Ibid.*, pp.170-2.

3.   Waltham Forest Archives: W47.1/2, pp.20-1; W83.1 R2, Parish Register, 1691-1733.

4.   Waltham Forest Archives: W47.1 Z1.

5.   Waltham Forest Archives: DA400 A2/13/9, Court Order, 29 November 1720.

6.   Waltham Forest Archives: DA400 A2/10/1, Will of Matthew Humberstone.

7.   Waltham Forest Archives: W47.1/1, p.75.

8.   William Houghton, *An Account of Benefactions in the Parish of St Mary, Walthamstow, in the County of Essex, Extracted from the Original Instruments, and Printed by Order of Vestry, held on 25 August 1876* (London, 1877), p.9.

9. *Ibid.*

10. John Coe, *An Account of Benefactions in the Parish of St Mary, Walthamstow, in the County of Essex, Extracted from the Original Instruments, by Order of Vestry, held on Tuesday, the 4th Day of April 1820* (London, 1821), p.8.

11. Waltham Forest Archives: DA400 A2/11/1, Will of Thomas Legendre; Coe, *An Account of Benefactions*, p.8.

12. Waltham Forest Archives: W47.1/3, p.24.

13. *Ibid.*, pp. 30-1.

14. Waltham Forest Archives: DA400 E2/20/1, Lease, 3 December 1728; Coe, *An Account of Benefactions*, p.7.

15. Waltham Forest Archives: DA400 A2/21/1, Declaration of Trust, 14 November 1783.

16. Waltham Forest Archives: DA400 A2/20/1, Will of Susan Samms.

17. This pamphlet has not survived; however, it is mentioned by Bosworth, *A History of Walthamstow Charities*, p.4.

18. Waltham Forest Archives: W47.1/4, p.137; DA400 A2/13/12, Release and Deed of Trust.

19. Waltham Forest Archives: W47.1/4, p.204.

20. *Ibid.*, pp.209-10, 215-17, 220-34, 236-7; Report of the Commissioners, pp.133-6; *see also* Bosworth, *A History of Walthamstow Charities*, pp.51-2.

21. Report of the Commissioners, p.137.

22. Waltham Forest Archives: W47.1/4, pp.410-11, 424, 427, 443.

23. Waltham Forest Archives: DA400 A2/23/1. (The original Deed of 30 and 31 October 1795 has not survived, but is recited in a draft Appointment of New Trustees dated 29 March 1856.)

24. Waltham Forest Archives: DA400 A2/23/1. (The original Deed of 3 November 1795 has not survived, but is recited in a draft Appointment of New Trustees dated 29 March 1856.) *See also* Waltham Forest Archives, DA400 Z1/4: Report of the Commissioners, pp.148-9.

25. Waltham Forest Archives: DA400 A2/23/1. (The Will of Mary Squire is recited in a draft Appointment of New Trustees dated 29 March 1856.) *See also* Waltham Forest Archives, DA400 Z1/4: Report of the Commissioners, pp.149-50.

26. Waltham Forest Archives, DA400 Z1/4: Report of the Commissioners, p.150; Bosworth, *A History of Walthamstow Charities*, p.40.

Chapter Seven: Reforming the System

1. 22 George III, c.83, clauses, 29-35, in *The Statutes at Large* (London, 1786) IX: 268-83.

2. Pauline Gregg, *A Social and Economic History of Britain 1760-1972*, 7th ed. (London, 1973), p.182.

3. Waltham Forest Archives: W55.61 P21-P65, Poor Rate Books.

4. Waltham Forest Archives: W47.1/5, pp. 354-25.

5. *Ibid.*, p.491.

6. Waltham Forest Archives: W34.41 M3, Workhouse Management Committee Minute Book, 20 May 1820 and 20 June 1820.

7. *Ibid.*, 10 October 1828.

8. *Ibid.*, 29 March 1829.

9. Report of the Royal Commission for inquiring into the Administration and practical Operation of the Poor Laws, 1834, XXII: 146, quoted in Gregg, *A Social and Economic History of Britain*, p.183.

10. *Ibid.*, XXIX, iii, 29, quoted in Gregg, p.183.

11. Waltham Forest Archives: W55.51 C3, Order of Poor Law Commissioners.

12. Waltham Forest Archives: W55.51 C4, Order of Poor Law Commissioners.

13. Waltham Forest Archives: W55.51 C7, correspondence file.

14. Waltham Forest Archives: W55.61 P65; W55.62 P1, Poor Rate Books.

15. P.H. Reaney and Hilda Grieve, 'Walthamstow', in W.R. Powell, ed., *A History of the County of Essex* (Oxford University Press, 1973), VI: 278-79.

16. Gregg, *A Social and Economic History of Britain*, p.495.

17. Quoted in Bosworth, *A History of Walthamstow Charities*, p.3.

18. *Abstract of the Returns of Charitable Donations for the Benefit of Poor Persons Made by the Ministers and Churchwardens of the Severall Parishes and Townships in England and Wales, 1786-1788. Ordered, by The House of Commons, to be Printed, 26 June 1816.* Volume I, pp. iv, 356-7.

19. *Burke's Peerage and Baronetage*, 89th ed. (1931), s.v. 'Brougham'; *Encyclopedia Britannica* 11th ed. (1910), s.v. 'Charity and Charities'.

20. Waltham Forest Archives: DA400 A1/5/1, Inventory.

21. Parliamentary Papers, Report of the Commissioners for Inquiring Concerning Charities, XVIII (1833): 129-74.

22. *Ibid.*, pp.136-7.

23. *Ibid.*, pp.154, 160, 165, 172-3.

24. Waltham Forest Archives: DA400 F1/1/2, Annual Charity Reports, 1852-1857.

Chapter Eight: The 19th-Century Charities

1. Waltham Forest Archives: DA400 A2/9/1, Deed Poll, 15 March 1782.

2. Report of the Commissioners, pp.153-4.

3. Waltham Forest Archives: DA400 A2/9/2, Letter, 25 April 1807.

4. Waltham Forest Archives: DA400 A2/3/1, Will of Willam Cluff.

5. Houghton, *An Account of Benefactions*, p.15.

6. Report of the Commissioners, p.165.

7. Waltham Forest Archives: DA400 A2/1/1, Will of Elizabeth Cass.

8. Bosworth, *A History of Walthamstow Charities*, p.43.

9. Waltham Forest Archives: DA400 A2/15/1, Will of John Morley.

10. Waltham Forest Archives: DA400 A2/15/2, Correspondence; DA400 A2/15/3, Bill of Complaint.

11. Report of the Commissioners, p.157.

12. Bosworth, *A History of Walthamstow Charities*, p.48; Waltham Forest Archives: DA400 E2/11/1, 3-7, Charity Commission Sealed Orders.

13. Coe, *An Account of Benefactions*, p.11.

14. Report of the Commissioners, p.138.

15. *Ibid.*; Waltham Forest Archives: W47.1/5, pp.488-9.

16. Report of the Commissioners, p.138.

17. Waltham Forest Archives: DA400 A2/4/1, Will of Elizabeth Collard.

18. Waltham Forest Archives: DA400 A2/23/1, Draft Appointment of Trustees.

19. Houghton, *An Account of Benefactions*, p.10.

20. Waltham Forest Archives: DA400 A2/6/1, Memorandum.

21. Waltham Forest Archives: DA400 A1/1/2, Charity Commission Scheme, p.18.

22. Waltham Forest Archives: DA400 E2/3F/5, Appointment and Conveyance.

23. Houghton, *An Account of Benefactions*, p.13; 'Mr. Houghton and Mrs. Collard's Charity', *The Walthamstow and Leyton Guardian*, 31 December 1881, p.5.

24. Waltham Forest Archives: DA400 E2/3A/1, Conveyance, 18 November 1889; DA400 E2/3B/1, Sealed Order, 6 January 1885; DA400 E2/3C/1, Sealed Order, 6 July 1883.

25. *Abstract of the Returns of Charitable Donations for the Benefit of Poor Persons Made by the Ministers and Churchwardens of the Severall Parishes and Townships in England and Wales, 1786-1788. Ordered, by The House of Commons, to be Printed, 26 June 1816.* Volume I, p. iv; Houghton, *An Account of Benefactions*, p.19; Waltham Forest Archives: DA400 A1/1/2, Charity Commission Scheme, pp.16-20.

Chapter Nine: Walthamstow Charity Governors

1. Waltham Forest Archives: DA400 F1/1/1, Charity Account Book, 1877-1895.

2. Waltham Forest Archives: W55.11 P140, West Ham Poor Law Union Quarterly Abstract.

3. *The Walthamstow and Leyton Guardian*, 20 July 1878, p.2.

4. Waltham Forest Archives; W34.42 R5 and W34.42 R6, West Ham Poor Law Union Relief Lists.

5. Waltham Forest Archives: W55.62 P1-48, Poor Rate Books, 1839-1874.

6. 'The Walthamstow Charities', *The Walthamstow and Leyton Guardian*, 25 November 1876.

7. 'The Walthamstow Charities Inquiry', *The Walthamstow and Leyton Guardian*, 16 December 1876.

8. Waltham Forest Archives: DA400 A2/14/5, letter, 4 December 1871.

9. 'The Local Charities', *The Walthamstow Chronicle*, 29 April 1876; 'Vestry Meeting', *The Walthamstow and Leyton Guardian*, 2 September 1876, pp.2-3; William Houghton, *An Account of Benefactions in the Parish of St Mary* (London: Printed by G. Mitton, 1877), pp.17-19.

10. 'The Walthamstow Charities', *The Walthamstow and Leyton Guardian*, 21 October 1876, p.2.

11. 'The Walthamstow Charities Inquiry', *The Walthamstow and Leyton Guardian*, 25 November, 2, 9, 16, 23 and 30 December 1876.

12. 'Walthamstow Charities', *The Walthamstow and Leyton Guardian*, 17, 24 and 31 March 1877.

13. 'Charitable Bequests in Walthamstow', *The Walthamstow and Leyton Guardian*, 13 May 1876.

14. Waltham Forest Archives: DA400 A1/1/1, Charity Commission Scheme, 30 April 1880.

15. Waltham Forest Archives: DA400 F1/1/9, Accounts, 30 April 1881.

16. Waltham Forest Archives: DA400 A1/2C/1, Polling Papers.

17. Waltham Forest Archives: DA400 A1/1/1, Charity Commission Scheme, 30 April 1880.

18. Waltham Forest Archives: DA400 A2/14/5, Charity Commission Scheme, 9 September 1884.

19. 'The Monoux Grammar School', *The Walthamstow and Leyton Guardian*, 25 July 1891, p.6.

20. Waltham Forest Archives: DA400 A2/13/16, Charity Commission Sealed Order, 16 April 1886.

21. Waltham Forest Archives: W55.1 C141.

22. *The Walthamstow Guardian*, 1 June 1923.

23. Waltham Forest Archives: W83.1 R2, transcript from register of George Montaign, Bishop of London, 18 December 1624.

24. 'Vestry Meeting at Walthamstow', *The Walthamstow and Leyton Guardian*, 16 August 1890, p.6.

25. 'The Walthamstow Charities', *The Walthamstow and Leyton Guardian*, 25 July 1891, pp.5-6; 'Report on Walthamstow Churchwardens' Charity Accounts for Year ending May 1890, by The Committee appointed by the Walthamstow Vestry on 14 August 1890, and Presented to the Vestry, 22 July 1891'; and 'Report on Walthamstow Charity Governors' and Mrs. Jane Sabina Collard's Charity Accounts for Year ending 30 April 1890, by The Committee appointed by the Walthamstow Vestry on 14 August 1890, and Presented to the Vestry, 23 July 1891.'

26. Waltham Forest Archives: 55.11 C142; 'Uproarious Vestry Meeting at the Town Hall', *The Walthamstow and Leyton Guardian*, 31 October 1891, pp.5-6; 'Mr. W. Houghton's Victory', *The Walthamstow and Leyton Guardian*, 7 November 1891, p.5.

27. 'Walthamstow Public Charities', *The Walthamstow and Leyton Guardian*, 13 February 1892, pp.5-7; 20 February 1892, pp.5-7; and 27 February 1892, p.6.

28. 'Walthamstow Public Charities', *The Walthamstow and Leyton Guardian*, 13 February 1892, p.6.

29. Waltham Forest Archives: DA400 A1/1/2, Charity Commission Scheme, 4 October 1895.

Chapter Ten: Walthamstow Parochial Charities

1. Waltham Forest Archives: DA400 A1/1/2, Charity Commission Scheme, 4 October 1895.

2. Waltham Forest Archives: DA400 A1/1/3, Charity Commission Scheme, 5 June 1908.

3. Waltham Forest Archives: DA400 A1/1/4, Charity Commission Scheme, 27 February 1914.

4. Waltham Forest Archives: DA400 F1/1/10, Charity Governors' Accounts.

5. Waltham Forest Archives: DA400 A1/3/1-4, Applications for New Year's Gift.

6. Waltham Forest Archives: DA400 A1/3/5, Bread Tickets.

7. Waltham Forest Archives: DA400 F1/1/1, Churchwardens' Account Book, 1877-1895.

8. Waltham Forest Archives: DA400 A1/3/6, Register of Pensioners, 1896-1962.

9. Pauline Gregg, *A Social and Economic History of Britain 1760-1972*, p.490; Waltham Forest Archives: DA400 A1/1/4, Charity Commission Scheme, 27 February 1914.

10. Waltham Forest Archives: DA400 A2/26/1, Charity Commission Scheme, 28 March 1924.

11. Waltham Forest Archives: DA400 A2/26/2, Register of Pensioners, 1924-1962; DA400 F2/6/1, Pension Account Book, 1944-1949.

12. Waltham Forest Archives: DA 400 A2/26/1 and DA400 A2/26/3, Charity Commission Scheme, 7 March 1952.

13. Waltham Forest Archives: DA400 A2/7/1, Declaration of Trust, 3 January 1925.

14. Waltham Forest Archives: DA400 A2/7/2, Charity Commission Scheme, 11 July 1952.

15. Waltham Forest Archives: DA400 A2/25/1, Charity Commission Scheme, 8 March 1955.

16. Waltham Forest Archives: DA400 A1/5/5, Application Forms, and DA400 F1/6/4, Voucher.

17. British Library: Additional MS 18783, Leiger Book of Estates of George Monoux, 1508-1553, f.6r, col. 1.

18. Waltham Forest Archives: DA400 A2/11/1, Extract from Will.
19. Waltham Forest Archives: DA400 A2/23/1, Draft Appointment of Trustees.
20. Waltham Forest Archives: DA400 A2/3/1, Extract from Will.
21. Waltham Forest Archives: DA400 A2/26/1, Charity Commission Scheme, 28 March 1924.
22. Waltham Forest Archives: DA400 A1/2C/5, Register of Trustees, back pages used for scrapbook of newspaper cuttings of notices, 1931-1955.
23. Waltham Forest Archives: DA400 A2/22/1, Minute Book, 1830-1835.
24. Waltham Forest Archives: E2/14/3, Enfranchisement, 22 December 1924, and DA400 E2/14/4, Duplicate Conveyance, 24 May 1939
25. Waltham Forest Archives: DA400 A2/22/8, Charity Commission Scheme, 7 February 1941.
26. Waltham Forest Archives: DA400 F1/1/15, Annual Report, 25 December 1942.

Chapter Eleven: Walthamstow Almshouse and General Charities

1. Waltham Forest Archives: DA400 E2/13/2, Conveyance, 24 December 1907.
2. Waltham Forest Archives: DA400 A1/1/8, Charity Commission Scheme, 22 March 1957, clause 4.
3. *Ibid.*, clauses 5-7.
4. Waltham Forest Archives: DA400 A1/1/5, Charity Commission Scheme, 28 March 1924.
5. Pauline Gregg, *A Social and Economic History of Britain 1760-1972*, p.504.
6. Waltham Forest Archives: DA400 A1/1/8, Charity Commission Scheme, 22 March 1957, clause 34.
7. Waltham Forest Archives: DA400 F1/1/19-54 and Annual Reports of the Walthamstow Almshouse and General Charities, 1997-1999.
8. Waltham Forest Archives: DA400 F1/1/19-54 and Annual Reports of the Walthamstow Almshouse and General Charities, 1997-1999.
9. Waltham Forest Archives: DA400 A1/3/8, newspaper cutting, 11 October 1968.
10. Waltham Forest Archives: DA400 A1/2A/18, Minutes of the Trustees.
11. Waltham Forest Archives: DA400 A1/1/8, Charity Commission Scheme, 22 March 1957, clause 34.
12. Waltham Forest Archives: DA400 A2/23/1, Draft Appointment of Trustees.
13. Waltham Forest Archives: DA400 A1/1/2, Charity Commission Scheme, 4 October 1895, p.19.
14. Waltham Forest Archives: DA400 A1/1/2, Charity Commission Scheme, 4 October 1895, clause 35.
15. Waltham Forest Archives: DA400 P2/2/3, Contract, 12 August 1908; Sealed Order, 12 February 1909.
16. Waltham Forest Archives: DA400 P2/2/15, Charity Commission letter, 20 August 1954.
17. Waltham Forest Archives: DA400 P2/2/7, Architect's Specification and Plans.
18. Waltham Forest Archives: DA400 P2/2/10, Architect's Report and Plans.
19. Waltham Forest Archives: DA400 P2/2/15, Letter, 20 August 1954; P2/2/16, Sealed Order, 26 November 1954; P2/2/17, Correspondence File.
20. Waltham Forest Archives: DA400 P2/2/15, Charity Commission letter, 20 August 1954.
21. Waltham Forest Archives: DA400 F1/1/19-54 and Annual Reports of the Walthamstow Almshouse and General Charities, 1997-1999.

22. Waltham Forest Archives: DA400 A1/1/8, Charity Commission Scheme, 22 March 1957, Clause 43.

23. Waltham Forest Archives: DA400 A1/2A/13, Trustees Minutes.

24. Waltham Forest Archives: DA400 F1/1/19-54 and Annual Reports of the Walthamstow Almshouse and General Charities, 1997-1999.

25. Waltham Forest Archives: DA400 A1/1/8, Charity Commission Scheme, 22 March 1957, clause 38.

26. Waltham Forest Archives: DA400 P2/2/19, Architect's Report and Plans.

27. Waltham Forest Archives: DA400 F1/1/19-22, Annual Reports, 1960-1963.

28. Waltham Forest Archives: DA400 P2/2/22-23, Sealed Orders, 25 July 1961; P2/2/25, Sealed Order, 3 October 1962.

29. Waltham Forest Archives: DA400 E2/3D/1, Surveyor's Report.

30. Waltham Forest Archives: DA400 E2/3D/2, Conveyance, 14 December 1966; DA400 E2/3D/4, Land Certificate, 17 April 1967; DA400 E2/3D/5, Land Certificate, 17 April 1967; E2/3D/9, Land Certificate, 4 March 1969; DA400 E2/3D/10, Land Certificate, 13 November 1970.

31. Waltham Forest Archives: DA400 P2/1/8, Architect's Plans, December 1969, and DA400 P2/1/9, Architect's Plans, November 1971.

32. Waltham Forest Archives: DA400 P2/1/10, Charity Commission Sealed Order, 18 May 1873, and DA400 P2/1/11, Contract, 22 May 1973.

33. Waltham Forest Archives: DA400 P2/1/13, Correspondence File.

34. Waltham Forest Archives: DA400 A2/23/2, Sealed Order, 7 April 1975; DA400 P2/3/3, Specification and Plans; and DA400 E2/7A/15, Sealed Order, 3 July 1974.

35. Waltham Forest Archives: DA400 A1/1/9, Charity Commission Scheme, 16 April 1974; and A1/1/10, Sealed Order, 30 April 1975.

36. Waltham Forest Archives: DA400 P2/2/27, Contract, 21 July 1977.

37. Waltham Forest Archives: DA400 R2/2/4, Counterpart Agreement, 7 July 1966; and P2/2/28, Contract, June 1979.

Chapter Twelve: Financing the Future

 1. Waltham Forest Archives: DA400 A2/12/1, Charity Commission Scheme, 18 July 1958.

 2. Waltham Forest Archives: DA400 A2/19/1, Deed of Release, 24 December 1969.

 3. WAGC Correspondence File 121, Letter, 23 May 1985.

 4. WAGC Correspondence File 121.

 5. Waltham Forest Archives: DA400 A2/24/1, Charity Commission Scheme, 15 January 1975.

 6. Waltham Forest Archives: DA400 A2/2A/1, Charity Commission Scheme, 21 June 1957.

 7. Waltham Forest Archives: DA400 A2/2C/1, Trustees Minutes.

 8. Waltham Forest Archives: DA400 A2/2A/2, Charity Commission Scheme, 5 February 1960.

 9. Waltham Forest Archives: DA400 A2/2A/4, Charity Commission Sealed Order, 6 November 1975; DA400 A2/2A/6, Charity Commission Sealed Order, 22 August 1979.

10. Waltham Forest Archives: DA400 A2/2C/1, Trustees Minutes; DA400 A2/2D/2, Correspondence File.

11. Waltham Forest Archives: DA400 A2/2C/1, Trustees Minutes.

12. Waltham Forest Archives: DA400 A2/2A/7, Charity Commission Scheme, 16 June 1980.

13. Waltham Forest Archives: DA400 F1/1/19-54, Annual Reports. 1960-1996.

14. Sir Robert Megarry and H.W.R. Wade, *The Law of Real Property*, 5th ed. (Stevens and Sons, 1984), pp.1127-32.

15. Waltham Forest Archives: DA400 E2/3E/2-13, Charity Commission Sealed Orders; DA400 P2/1/10, Charity Commission Sealed Order, 18 May 1973.

16. Waltham Forest Archives: A1/1/8, Charity Commission Sealed Order, 22 March 1957, pp. 9, 11; DA400 E2/3E/2-13; DA400 E2/20/45-66, Charity Commission Sealed Orders and Correspondence.

Index